序

　　中國菜有很多烹調方法－蒸、煮、炒、燴…
等，不論用那種方法常常會把廚房弄得烏烟瘴氣
，因此很多人一提到中國式廚房，直覺地就認為
是窄小、悶熱、多種味道又油膩，使得很多家庭
主婦想到作菜及其善後的清潔工作就頭痛不已。

　　微波爐是一種既方便又可保持環境清潔的加
熱器。傳統在廚房工作時，由於電爐或瓦斯爐的
加熱，常會在無形中增高溫度，以致汗流浹背；
而微波爐最大好處就在於不會使環境的溫度升高
。又微波爐的加熱作業均在固定容器之內，因此
雖然在進行爆香、煎、烤等過程時，也不會濺得
到處都是油；節省不少清理的工作及時間。所以
，雖然有時用微波爐作菜的時間與瓦斯爐相同，
但是好處却較多。

　　一般人買了微波爐之後，只用來加熱剩菜，
或煮開水而已，總認為微波爐做中國菜味道不好
，因此味全文教基金會研究組以一年多的時間不
斷地研究，希望利用微波爐的優點，做出可口的
中國菜。

　　在這本微波爐食譜裏，我們不但向各位介紹
微波爐的烹調用具、簡單的使用方法及保養要訣
，同時也推出六十二道精心製作的主菜、副菜及
點心，這些菜餚均經過多次的試驗及很多消費者
的品評才告完成，我們簡化每道菜的作法，但烹
調出來的菜餚仍不失其風味。

　　對於現代忙碌的家庭主婦，尤其是上班族，
想要在短時間內，讓一家人能享受到香噴噴的飯
菜，用微波爐作菜該是最恰當不過了。

Preface

Many methods of cooking are used in Chinese cuisine: steaming, boiling, stir-frying, cooking in sauce, and so forth; but no matter what method is used, the kitchen usually ends up full of oily steam. The impression most people have of a Chinese kitchen is a crowded, hot, stuffy place full of all kinds of cooking smells — and greasy. Just thinking about cooking and the chores that follow is enough to give anyone a headache.

The microwave oven is an instrument for heating food that is both convenient and clean. Cooking with conventional gas or electric stoves often results in a significant rise in room temperature, creating discomfort for anyone nearby. One of the biggest advantages of microwave cooking is that it does not raise room temperature. With a microwave, the actual cooking takes place in a restricted area, so the kitchen does not become grease-spattered during flash-frying, pan-frying, and baking. This saves a tremendous amount of cleanup time and work. So even if actual cooking time is sometimes the same with a microwave as with a conventional range, the microwave still offers a lot of other advantages.

People who buy microwave ovens often end up using them mostly for warming up leftovers or boiling water; they feel that a microwave is not suitable for making Chinese food. It is for this reason that the Wei-Chuan Educational and Cultural Foundation devoted over one year to researching and testing how to incorporate the advantages of microwave cooking into making delicious Chinese food.

In this book, we introduce the basic implements of microwave cooking, how to care for a microwave, and 62 specially selected main dishes, side dishes, and snacks. Each recipe was tested several times in our test kitchens, then retested and evaluated by a large number of consumers before being chosen for inclusion in this book. Each recipe was simplified as much as possible while preserving the original taste and character of the dish.

Busy people, especially those who work outside the home, will find the microwave oven a most useful piece of equipment in preparing delicious homemade Chinese food in the shortest amount of time.

Lee Hwa Lin

微波爐的秘密

　　微波爐是以電波來加熱的器具，電波的種類很多，微波爐所用的電波是UHF電視所用的，也是雷達所用的電波的一種。當然這種電波與電視或通信所用者，其波長有差異，以免通訊設備等受到干擾。

　　微波爐加熱的原理是利用食物所含的水分等極性物質的特性來加熱。在微波爐內，磁場會以很快的速度改變，而像水等極性物質會被電波所振動，使分子間互相摩擦發熱。好比在冬天時，我們將雙手互相摩擦使其發熱取暖一樣。這種現象也會在食物中發生，所以在水份、油脂等存在的地方漸漸熱起來。另外微波加熱與傳統加熱不同的地方，是被微波加熱的食物會自中心部分熱起來，而非由外面熱到裡面。

　　電波可以通過紙張、木頭(已乾燥者)、塑膠或陶器之類的東西，因此，裝於紙盒的食物，或裝於磁器內的食物，可直接放入微波爐加熱。但裝於鋁箔材料等器皿之食物卻無法加熱，因為鋁箔或罐頭的鐵皮等會反射電波。

　　在使用微波爐時要特別小心，如果加熱的東西中含有金屬膜或金屬板之類，則如前述會反射其電波，不但不能使裡面的東西熱起來，還會因金屬的存在，發出火花來。連繪有金邊的陶器或碗都會產生火花，細長的金屬被電波照射後，會使其帶電，因而發出火花。因此，繪有金線或銀線的碗碟會由於帶電，發出火花，而最後使這部分掉下來，掉下來的金屬屑片會散在食物內，因此有被食用的可能。

　　另外，要特別小心釘書機的鐵釘。市售的食品常以釘書機的鐵釘來固定或封口，如不小心將其放入微波爐內加熱，不但會發生火花，火花還會掉到袋子上，使其燃燒起來。

　　如將整個蛋或整條香蕉放入加熱，即會破裂把微波爐內部弄髒，這是因為蛋黃帶有膜，香蕉有皮包起來，會因加熱而水蒸氣無法散發會引起爆炸。如在菜湯中放入蛋(未經打散者)，而給與微波加熱，也會發生不可收拾的後果。

　　以微波爐加熱的甘諸不會甜，這是因為加熱過於迅速，使甘諸中的酵素無暇作用，因此糖分不會增加。

　　另外，如以微波爐將澱粉食品加熱，在冷却後會感覺乾且硬。因此在加熱時，最好以保鮮膜等包起來，並且應該趁熱食用。

　　像漢堡、鷄腿或輪切的魚肉等，如要烘烤則需要很久的時間，且很難使中心部分熟透。而且如單以微波爐加熱，無法使外皮呈金黃色且酥脆並發出焦香來。這種食物可先烘烤其表面，然後再以微波爐加熱。現在已有裝有微波及紅外線(或電熱線) 二種熱源裝置的烤爐出售。

微波爐的最大用處是食物的加熱，尤其是加熱菜餚最好用。但要注意的是，以保鮮膜或塑膠材料包裝的油炸食物在微波爐內加熱時，食物本身的溫度會昇得很高，往往會超過塑膠材料的可耐溫度，而引起塑膠材料的變形、溶出等，食用這種食物可能對人體有害，所以要小心。

在乾燥方面，微波爐也能發揮其效力。如已潮濕的餅乾、柴魚屑、海苔等都可使用微波爐很快地乾燥。

沒有澀味蔬菜的前處理，如利用微波爐則很方便。將蔬菜以保鮮膜包起來，放入微波爐加熱即可。如此不但可保持翠綠的顏色，其甜味也不會流失，維生素C含量也高。但要注意的是加熱後，要立即加以冷卻，不然顏色會轉劣。

微波爐也可以用來解凍。但是微波爐對於冰層的滲透較水為慢，所以對於較厚的食物，常會發生外部已熟了，但內部依然冰冷的現象。較高級的微波爐則裝有解凍用按鈕，這是照射食物一段時間，停止一段時間，然後再給予加熱的裝置。其目的是要讓熱量先滲透、平衡以後，再反覆加熱、停止、平衡的作用。

微波加熱的原理是靠食物所含的極性成分震動來發熱的，因此，由於不同極性的成分，其發熱的程度也不一樣，如將一塊肉放入加熱，肥肉會較瘦肉熱一點。又，像水雖然能被加熱，但溫度卻始終不能高至攝氏一百度。

因為微波加熱的方式與傳統加熱不同，所以不能用普通的水銀或酒精溫度計來測定爐內的溫度。如將普通的溫度計放入微波爐內加熱，溫度計可能會炸破。

微波爐是一種既方便，又可保持乾淨的加熱器，它又不會使環境溫度升高，所以裝冷氣的環境非常適合使用。

在經濟上，微波爐與傳統加熱，那一種省電呢？微波會有效地被轉變為熱能，不過由電能轉成微波效率較差，所以微波雖然較電熱器省電，相差卻不大。

很多人對微波爐的安全性抱有懷疑的態度，其實微波爐在設計時，都已顧慮到安全性。例如微波爐的門附有安全裝置，門一打開後，爐本身的電源就會自動關掉。另外，微波如有漏洩，碰到人體就會有熱感，所以使用時不至於有危險。

The Secrets of Microwave Cooking

A microwave oven uses electric waves to heat food. There are many different kinds of electric waves; the kind used by a microwave are in the ultra high frequency (UHF) range, the same as those used in television broadcasting and radar. Of course, oven microwaves are of a different length than those used for television signals, so there is no interference between the two.

The microwave heating process depends on the special properties of polarized materials, such as water, contained in the food to be heated. Magnetic fields reverse back and forth at great speed inside a microwave oven to produce electric waves, which set polarized material such as water and fat into a rapid vibration. This causes the molecules to produce heat from friction, in much the same way as when we rub our hands together quickly to create warmth through friction on a cold day. Another way in which microwave cooking differs from conventional heating methods is that a microwave heats food from the inside out, rather than from the outside in.

Electric waves can pass through wood, plastic, and ceramics, so foods in cardboard or china containers can be placed directly into the microwave oven for heating. Foods wrapped or contained in aluminum foil, however, cannot be warmed in a microwave because electric waves bounce off foil and metal. For this reason, you must be especially careful not to use containers that have a metal coating or metal base plate. Not only will the food not become heated because of wave deflection; the presence of metal will also cause sparks to fly in the oven. Even a gold or silver border on ceramic dishes or china will carry a current and produce sparks. The border will as a result flake off and scatter into the food, and possibly be ingested.

Be also very careful of metal staples, often used to secure food pckaging. If a staple is inadvertantly heated in a microwave oven it will not only produce sparks, but the sparks may fall onto the wrapping and ignite it.

Heating a whole fresh egg with or without the shell or a whole banana in a microwave oven will cause the food to burst and splatter all over the oven interior. This is because there is a membrane surrounding the egg yolk and an enclosing skin on the banana. When either of these items is heated, steam builds up and is trapped inside with no way of escaping; the food then bursts open. If a whole unbeaten egg is added to a soup and then heated in a microwave oven, you will have a big clean-up job when you remove it.

Yams or sweet potatoes baked in a microwave oven do not come out very sweet. This is because the heating process is so rapid that the enzymes in the sweet potato do not have time to convert the starch into sugar.

After cooling, the texture of starchy foods heated in a microwave oven will become hard and dry. This is because during the cooking process the water molecules in the food are made to vibrate intensely, leave the cells of the food, and evaporate. The best way to work around this drawback is to cover the food with plastic wrap while cooking, and to eat the food while still hot.

Thick, dense foods such as hamburgers, chicken legs, and fish fillets require long cooking times, and it is difficult to get them thoroughly done inside. And there is no way to brown and crisp these foods on the outside using only a microwave oven. This type of food can be first surface browned in a conventional oven, or fried, then heated in a microwave to complete the cooking process. Ovens are now available with both microwave and infrared (or electric heat element) functions.

Microwave ovens are most useful in warming or reheating food. You must, however, take special care when using a microwave to reheat deep fried foods wrapped in plastic. The food temperature will become very high, often going beyond the heat resistance level of the plastic wrap. The plastic wrap may then become misshapen or melt. This may cause the release of harmful substances into the food.

The microwave is also useful for its drying function. Crackers, cookies, dried fish, dry seaweed, and other dry foods that have become soggy can be quickly dried out and freshened in a microwave oven.

Blanching fresh vegetables with a microwave is especially convenient. All you need to do is wrap the vegetables in plastic wrap and heat in the microwave oven. Not only do they retain their bright green color, but also their natural fresh taste and high vitamin C content. But remember to cool the vegetables immediately after cooking, or they will become discolored.

A microwave can also be used to defrost frozen food. However, because microwave heat penetrates ice more slowly than water, the food to be defrosted may become cooked on the outside while the center remains icy. More sophisticated microwave ovens have a special defrost function. It heats for a while, stops, then heats again. This permits the the heat to penetrate slowly and evenly throughout the whole food item.

A microwave heats food by setting its polarized molecules into rapid vibration. Some materials contain greater or less proportions of polarized molecules, and as a result, heat to different temperatures. If a piece of meat is heated in a microwave, the fat portion will become hotter than the lean. And although water can be heated in a microwave, it can never be brought to its 100°C (212°F) boiling point.

Because the method by which microwave ovens heat food differs from conventional ovens, mercury or alcohol thermometers cannot be used inside a microwave to measure interior temperature; the thermometer might explode.

Microwave cooking is both clean and convenient. Because it does not raise the indoor room temperature, it is well suited for use in air-conditioned areas.

Is a microwave more economical to use than a conventional oven? Although microwaves are efficiently converted into heat energy, electric power is not as efficiently converted into microwaves. For this reason, microwave cooking uses less electricity than a conventional oven, but the difference is not a great one.

A lot of people have reservations about the safety of microwave use. This is unnecessary. All the needed safety features have been designed and built into the microwave oven. The door of a microwave, for example, has the feature of shutting off the main power source if the door is opened. If ever a leak of microwave energy occurs, it can be perceived as heat and easily discovered. So use your microwave with confidence and assurance.

Chin Fang Li

微波爐的功能

微波爐具有多種功能，除可蒸煮煎炸食物之外，亦可當烤箱使用。電力在五百瓦以下的較合適再熱食物，六百瓦以上的烹調功能較佳，本書是以七百瓦電力的微波爐烹調食物，如果沒有特別指出，則以強度100％加熱。

以下即介紹微波爐的三種主要功能：

一、解凍

　　將冷凍食物置碗盤內加蓋，或裝于耐熱袋內，用解凍鍵或30％的電力來解凍，並隨時查看，以免解凍過度而煮熟。

二、再熱

　　通常以HI或REHEAT進行再熱，再熱後的食物應立即食用，以免冷卻後食物變乾硬。如果食物表面已有乾硬現象，應先灑點水，再覆耐熱膜加熱約30秒。麵包、點心、油炸物再熱時，最好在底部墊紙巾，以便吸油。

三、烹飪

　　利用微波爐的特性，配合各類器皿，發揮煎煮炒烤等多項烹飪功能。

　　烹飪要領：

　　1.肉餡或泥狀的餡需將表面抹勻，使受熱均勻。烹煮食物時，材料要儘量攤開，增加接觸面，使作用較快。另須注意烹飪時間，以免食物燒焦。食物煮熟後，稍微再燜一下，可使熱量繼續傳導至內部，讓烹調更完全。長時間烹調時，於中途拿出來攪拌，再繼續加熱，可縮短烹飪時間。

　　2.由於微波的烹煮作用是由內往外熱，因此最好將小塊易熟者置盤子內側，質地厚者置外側。上下放置食物時，應交錯排列勿重疊。

　　3.因為蔬菜蓬鬆佔空間，所以炒青菜時要用廣口的深器皿，以免蔬菜掉落盤外，無法烹調。若是蔬菜洗好後立即烹煮，則不必灑水，直接拌油加調味料即可。如果蔬菜已瀝乾水份，則需在加熱前略灑些水。

　　4.烹調多汁或湯類的食物，儘量利用高湯或熱開水，可縮短烹飪時間；且最好以廣口深器皿盛裝，並在容器下墊一盤子，防止湯汁溢出，弄髒微波爐。

　　5.以耐熱膜代替蓋子時，勿封得太緊或在膜上戳洞，以免耐熱膜脹破，水蒸氣溢出。如食物含油太多時，勿使用耐熱膜，因一般耐熱膜只耐熱130°C，而油溫通常高於130°C，易使耐熱膜熔化。有下列情形時，切記勿使用耐熱膜或加蓋：①熱油②爆香③勾芡④煎烤⑤烤盤預熱⑥特殊目的，例如收汁。

　　6.烤雞腿時為免汁液沾上烤盤，可將鋁箔紙的反面舖於烤盤上。

　　7.烹煮蛋類不宜用HI電力，以免導致蛋的質地粗糙；最好改用較小的電力，如BRAISE或MEDIUM(60％～70％的電力)。另帶殼的全蛋不可入微波爐烹煮，不帶殼的全蛋需用牙籤將蛋黃膜戳幾個洞，以防止蛋黃膜爆裂，濺滿微波爐。

The Functions of a Microwave Oven

A microwave oven can perform a number of different functions. In addition to steaming, boiling, pan frying, and deep frying food, it can also function as an oven. Microwaves with 500W or less of power are best suited to reheating food; 600W or more is generally required for cooking. A 700W microwave was used in developing the recipes for this book.

Below are described the three main functions of a microwave:

1. Thawing and defrosting: Place the food item to be defrosted in a dish and cover, or place in a heat-resistant bag. Use the "DEFROST" button or 30% power to defrost food. Check the food frequently while it is being thawed in the microwave to make sure that it is not being "overthawed", i.e. cooked.

2. Reheating: The "HI" or "REHEAT" buttons are the ones usually used to reheat food. Serve and eat food items immediately after reheating to prevent the food from becoming hard and dry. If the surface of the food is already dry and hard, sprinkle a little water over it, cover with heat-resistant wrap, and heat another 30 seconds in the microwave. When reheating rolls, dim sum, or fried foods, place some paper towelling underneath to absorb the oil.

3. Cooking: The special features of the microwave, when matched with the appropriate food container, can allow you to pan fry, boil, stir-fry, bake, and so forth in your microwave with ease.

Points to remember when cooking with a microwave:

1. The surface of meat stuffings or other fillings and pastes must be made smooth before heating, so that the cooking will be even. Spread out the ingredients to be heated as much as possible to increase the surface area directly exposed to the microwaves. This will shorten cooking time. Also, monitor cooking time carefully so as to avoid burning or scorching the food. Leave the food item in the oven for a little while after the power shuts off; the heat will continue to penetrate to the interior of the food, thus completing the cooking process.

For long cooking times, remove the food item about halfway through the cooking process, and stir or turn over the food before returning it to the oven to finish cooking. This will shorten the total amount of cooking time required.

2. Because a microwave oven heats food from the inside out, it is best to place any small pieces, which will cook more quickly, towards the center of the oven, and thicker pieces on the outside or border edges. If cooking on two different vertical levels, arrange the food items in a staggered pattern; do not stack.

3. Because vegetables are light and bulky, cook them in a deep, wide-mouthed container to prevent them from falling off the dish to where they cannot be properly cooked. Cook vegetables immediately after washing; no extra water need be sprinkled over them. The oil and seasonings may be mixed right in, and the vegetable is ready to heat. If the vegetables have been well drained, sprinkle a little water over them before placing in the microwave to cook.

4. When cooking soups or food with a high moisture content, use soup stock or hot water for the liquid as much as possible; this will shorten cooking time. It is best to heat soups in a deep, wide-mouthed container, and to place a plate underneath the container while it is cooking, to prevent the liquid from boiling over and spilling onto the oven interior. If the food contains a large amount of oil or fat, do not use heat-resistant plastic wrap.

5. When using heat-resistant plastic wrap as a cover, do not stretch it too tautly or poke holes in it. This is to prevent the plastic wrap from bursting and the steam inside from escaping. Do not use heat-resistant plastic wrap when cooking food with a high fat content. Most heat-resistant plastic wrap can withstand temperatures only up to 130°C (266°F); but the temperature of fat heated in a microwave usually exceeds 130°C, and would melt most plastic wraps. Make sure not to use plastic wrap or any other kind of cover in the following cases: 1. heating oil; 2. frying ginger, garlic, or other condiments to flavor oil; 3. thickening a sauce with cornstarch; 4. pan frying; 5. preheating a baking dish; 6. special purposes, such as reducing a sauce.

6. When baking chicken legs, the baking dish may be lined with aluminum foil, dull side up, for easier cleanup.

7. Avoid using the "HI" setting on your microwave when cooking eggs, or the texture will become coarse and mealy. Lower settings, such as "BRAISE" or "MEDIUM" (60%-70% power) are preferable. Do not cook whole eggs still in the shell in a microwave. For eggs out of the shell, first prick the membrane of the yolk several times with a toothpick. This prevents the yolk from bursting and spattering all over the oven interior.

烹飪用具介紹及其保護方法

1. 耐熱膜：市面上的保鮮膜品牌甚多，選購時須注意產品外包裝標示，至少耐高溫120℃方可使用，若無耐熱膜，可以蒸年糕的玻璃紙代替。
2. 耐熱袋：以它來烹飪蔬菜類食品效果甚佳。爲防止其於烹飪時漲破，不可將袋口綁緊。
3. 陶瓷器：砂鍋及一般陶瓷碗盤不帶金銀邊者皆可使用。
4. 耐熱玻璃器皿：選購時將玻璃器皿迎向光線明亮處，不含氣泡且無雜質者都可使用。
5. 美耐皿類器皿：質地類似塑膠，須耐熱130℃以上方可使用。另此類器皿的蓋子分有保鮮蓋及專供烹飪使用者，不可誤用。
6. 塑膠容器：放入微波爐內以HI電力加熱15～20秒，若容器生溫熱者不得使用。
7. 木竹容器及紙類製品：只適合短時間快速加熱用，且其表面塗漆者不可使用。
8. 烤盤：微波爐專用烤盤之背面經過特殊材料處理，能吸收微波，將熱集中在盤子上，使食物經加熱產生焦黃的效果。烤盤在放入食物前，應先以HI電力空盤預熱四分鐘以上。預熱後，表面及底部均很熱，切勿用手觸摸，以免燙傷。若要將烤盤再預熱，應先將殘渣或餘汁清除至四周的溝槽內。烤盤不可用刀叉、尖銳利器刮傷，或以菜瓜布等粗糙的清潔品清洗，以免刮傷盤面。
9. 蒸盤：蒸盤上附有架子，置材料於架子上，或直接放於盤中蒸煮視情況而定，將盤中的架子拿出，亦可當一般盤子使用。
10. 感溫探針：用來測肉溫度。

Utensils and Utensil Care
for Microwave Cooking

1. Heat-resistant wrap: There are many brands of plastic wrap on the market. Check the label carefully to make sure the plastic wrap you choose can withstand temperatures of at least up to 120°C (248°F). If plastic wrap is unavailable, cellophane may be used instead.

2. Heat-resistant bags: These are good for cooking vegetables. Do not close tightly, to prevent bursting.

3. Ceramic, stoneware, and china: Clay pots, ceramic and stoneware, and china without a metallic border can be used in a microwave.

4. Heat-resistant glassware: When buying glassware for use in microwave cooking, hold it up to a light and examine it carefully. Buy only glassware that contains no air bubbles or extraneous matter.

5. Melamine-type dishware: Melamine, which is similar to plastic, must be heat resistant at temperatures up to 130°C (266°F) or higher. This type of dishware has two kinds of covers, one for storage and retaining freshness, and another for cooking use. Do not confuse the two.

6. Plasticware: Test plasticware before use by placing it in the microwave and heating it on the "HI" power setting for 15 to 20 seconds. If the container becomes warm to the touch, do not use it for microwave cooking.

7. Wood, bamboo, and paper containers: Containers made of these materials are suitable only for quick heating short periods of time in a microwave. Do not use painted or varnished containers.

8. Baking dishes: Baking dishes which are specifically designed for microwave use are made of materials that have been specially treated to absorb microwaves and concentrate heat in the container. This causes food to be browned. Before placing food in a baking dish, preheat the empty dish for four minutes or more on the "HI" power setting. The surfaces and bottom will become very hot, so do not touch the dish with your bare hands, or you may burn yourself. If you need to preheat the baking dish again, push all the remaining food and sauce in the dish into the "trough" along the edges. Do not use knives, forks, or other sharp or pointed objects in a microwave baking dish; and do not scrub it with scouring pads, steel wool, or other rough or harsh objects; they might scratch or otherwise damage the surface of the dish.

9. Steaming dish: Food to be steamed in a steaming dish is placed on the support, which rests in the water-filled dish. The food may in some cases be placed directly in the dish. Removing the support converts the steaming dish into a regular microwave dish.

10. Temperature monitor: This is used for monitoring the temperature of meat.

目錄 Contents

蛋、豆腐類 Eggs & Bean Curd

蔬菜類 Vegetables

湯類 Soup

點心類 Snacks and Sweets

火腿冬瓜夾

Wintermelon-Ham Pockets

材料：

冬瓜	⋯⋯⋯⋯⋯	300公克
火腿	⋯⋯⋯⋯⋯	30公克
葱	⋯⋯⋯⋯⋯	6段
油	⋯⋯⋯⋯⋯	2大匙

① { 水⋯⋯⋯⋯⋯3/4杯
  盐⋯⋯⋯⋯⋯1/2小匙
  糖、味精⋯各1/8小匙

② { 太白粉⋯⋯⋯ 1小匙
  水⋯⋯⋯⋯⋯ 1小匙

❶冬瓜去皮，囊切成4×6公分連刀片十二片（圖1）每片中間夾入一片火腿（圖2）備用。

❷葱洗淨切小段備用。

❸取一深盤入油2大匙預熱2分鐘，再爆香葱段1分鐘，隨入冬瓜夾及①料，加蓋（圖3）後續煮5分鐘最後入②料勾芡加熱20秒即可。

■ 採買冬瓜時請買厚度約4公分者，切成連刀片較為美觀。

INGREDIENTS:

300g (10½ oz.)		wintermelon
30g (1 oz.)		ham, cut into 12 thin slices
6 sections (1½'')		green onion
2 T.		cooking oil
①	¾ c.	water
	½ t.	salt
	⅛ t. each:	sugar, MSG
②	1 t.	cornstarch
	1 t.	water

❶ Peel the wintermelon. Cut into twelve 4×6 cm (1½'' ×2½'') slices, then split the slices open, leaving them jointed at the base (illus. 1). Insert one slice of ham into each pocket (illus. 2), and set aside.

❷ Wash the green onion and cut into 3.5 cm (1½'') sections. Set aside.

❸ Add 2 tablespoons oil to a deep baking dish and preheat for 2 minutes. Fry the green onion in the oil for another minute, then add the wintermelon-ham pockets and ①. Cover (illus. 3) and microwave for 5 minutes. Finally, add ② and heat for 20 seconds to thicken. Serve.

■ When buying the wintermelon, choose a piece that is about 4 cm (1⅔'') thick for best results.

揚州獅子頭 / Yangchow Style Lion's Head

材料：

青江菜	600公克		水	2杯
絞肉	370公克	②	酒、味精	各1小匙
荸薺	70公克		醬油　塩	各½小匙

①
- 蛋　　　　　　　1個
- 酒、醬油　各2小匙
- 葱末、薑末
- 　　　　　　　各1小匙
- 味精、塩　各¼小匙

❶ 荸薺剁碎去水，備用。

❷ 絞肉、荸薺及①料同方向拌勻（圖1），甩打數次，分四份做成肉丸備用。

❸ 青江菜洗淨對剖置砂鍋內（圖2），續入②料，加蓋後入微波爐加熱15分鐘，取出，上置肉丸（圖3），加蓋續熱20分鐘即可。

INGREDIENTS:

	600g (1⅓ lb.)	ching kang tsai, bok choy, or similar leafy green
	370g (13 oz.)	ground pork
	70g (2½ oz.)	water chestnuts
①	1	egg
	2 t. each:	cooking wine, soy sauce
	1 t. each:	minced green onion, minced ginger root
	¼ t. each:	MSG, salt
②	2 c.	water
	1 t. each:	cooking wine, MSG
	½ t. each:	soy sauce, salt

❶ Peel the water chestnuts (if using fresh), mince, use a cloth to squeeze out water, and set aside.

❷ Mix the ground pork, water chestnuts, and ① together thoroughly (illus. 1), always stirring in the same direction. Roll the meat mixture into a ball and throw against a counter or cutting board several times (this improves the texture). Divide into 4 portions and form into large meatballs Set aside.

❸ Wash the vegetable and cut in halves lengthwise. Arrange inside a clay pot (illus. 2). Add ②, cover, and microwave 15 minutes. Add the meatballs (illus. 3), cover, and heat another 20 minutes in the microwave. Serve.

吉利豬排

Pork Cutlet

材料：

		①		
里肌肉‥‥‥‥ 300公克		水‥‥‥‥‥‥‥ 2大匙
蛋‥‥‥‥‥‥‥‥ 1個		酒‥‥‥‥‥‥‥ 1大匙
麵包粉‥‥‥‥‥‥ 1杯		塩‥‥‥‥‥‥‥½小匙
太白粉‥‥‥‥‥‥¼杯		味精‥‥‥‥‥‥⅛小匙
油‥‥‥‥‥‥‥ 4大匙		胡椒粉‥‥‥‥‥‥少許

❶里肌肉剔除白筋（圖1）切成六片，再用肉鎚拍鬆（圖2），入①料拌醃20分鐘，備用。

❷蛋打散備用。

❸醃好的肉片依序沾上太白粉、蛋汁及麵包粉（圖3）備用。

❹油4大匙入烤盤，預熱5分鐘，放入三片吉利豬排，加熱1分30秒後，翻面續熱1分鐘，即可取出排在吸油紙上。

❺烤盤再熱2分鐘，放入剩餘的三片豬排，加熱1分30秒，翻面續熱1分鐘即可。

INGREDIENTS:

300g (⅔ lb.)		lean pork
1		egg
1 c.		fine bread crumbs
¼ c.		cornstarch
4 T.		cooking oil
①	2 T.	water
	1 T.	cooking wine
	½ t.	salt
	⅛ t.	MSG
	pinch of pepper	

❶ Remove the white sinews from the pork (illus. 1). Cut into 6 slices. Pound tender with a meat mallet (illus. 2). Add ① and marinate for 20 minutes. Set aside.

❷ Beat the egg lightly and set aside.

❸ Dip the pork slices first into the corn-starch, then into the beaten egg, and last into the fine bread crumbs (illus 3). Set aside.

❹ Add 4 tablespoons oil to a baking dish and preheat for 5 minutes. Arrange three pork cutlets in the dish, heat for 1 minute and 30 seconds, and turn over. Heat for another minute and remove. Drain on absorbent paper.

❺ Heat the baking dish for another two minutes. Arrange the three remaining pork cutlets in the dish. Microwave for 1 minute and 30 seconds. Turn over the meat, and heat for one more minute. Serve.

香菇盒子 / Stuffed Chinese Black Mushrooms

材料：

乾香菇…12朵（約30公克）	
絞肉…………… 200公克	
蝦仁………………80公克	
太白粉……………… 1小匙	
① 蛋白…………………½個 太白粉………… 1大匙 酒、薑末… 各1小匙 塩、醬油…各½小匙 麻油…………¼小匙 胡椒粉…………少許	② 高湯……………½杯 塩、糖……各½小匙 麻油、醬油…各少許 ③ 太白粉、水·各1小匙

❶香菇泡軟，擠乾水份備用。蝦仁洗淨抽去沙腸（圖1），剁成泥狀，與絞肉及①料拌勻成餡，再分成十二等份備用。

❷香菇上灑少許太白粉（圖2），鑲上一等份的餡（圖3），依序完成12個香菇盒子，排在盤子上，蓋上保鮮膜加熱5分鐘取出。

❸將②料蓋上保鮮膜加熱2分鐘，再入③料勾芡加熱30秒，取出淋在香菇盒子上即可。

INGREDIENTS:

12	dried Chinese black mushrooms (about 30g or 1 oz.)
200g (7 oz.)	ground pork
80g (3 oz.)	shelled shrimp
1 t.	cornstarch
① ½ 1 T. 1 t. each: ½ t. each: ¼ t. pinch of pepper	egg white cornstarch cooking wine, minced ginger root salt, soy sauce sesame oil
② ½ c. ½ t. each: dash each of sesame oil, soy sauce	soup stock salt, sugar
③ 1 t. each:	cornstarch, water

❶ Soak the dried Chinese black mushrooms until soft. Squeeze out the excess water and set aside. Wash the shrimp and devein (illus. 1). Chop into a paste and mix into the ground pork and ① until thoroughly blended. This is the stuffing. Divide the stuffing into 12 uniform portions and set aside.

❷ Sprinkle a small amount of cornstarch over the underside of the mushrooms (illus. 2). Press one portion of meat and shrimp stuffing firmly onto the underside of each of the 12 mushrooms (illus. 3). Arrange, stuffing side up, on a plate or platter, and cover with plastic wrap. Heat in the microwave for 5 minutes and remove.

❸ Heat ② in a plastic wrap-covered baking dish for 2 minutes, then add ③ and heat another 30 seconds to thicken. Remove and drizzle this sauce over the stuffed mushrooms. Serve.

魚香肉絲 / Szechuan Style Shredded Pork

材料：

里肌肉	300公克	水	4½大匙
木耳	60公克	醬油	2½大匙
荸薺	60公克	酒、油	各2大匙
油	3大匙	白醋	½大匙
葱末	少許	② 太白粉、糖	
① 葱末、薑末、蒜末‥			各1小匙
各1大匙		塩	¼小匙
辣豆瓣醬	1½小匙	味精、胡椒粉	
			各少許

❶里肌肉剔除白筋切細絲，入②料拌醃15分鐘備用。
❷木耳、荸薺切末後擠去水份（圖1）備用。
❸油3大匙預熱2分鐘，再爆香①料2分鐘（圖2），
　與醃好的肉絲、木耳末和荸薺末拌勻（圖3）續熱2
　分30秒，取出灑上葱末即可。

INGREDIENTS:

300g (⅔ lb.)		lean pork
60g (2 oz.)		wood ears (Chinese tree fungus)
60g (2 oz.)		water chestnuts
3 T.		cooking oil
chopped green onion, as desired		
①	1 T. each:	minced green onion, minced ginger root, minced garlic
	1½ t.	hot bean paste
②	4½ T.	water
	2½ T.	soy sauce
	2 T. each:	cooking wine, cooking oil
	½ T.	white rice vinegar
	1 t. each:	cornstarch, sugar
	¼ t.	salt
	pinch each of MSG and pepper	

❶ Remove the white sinews and shred the pork. Marinate in ② for 15 minutes and set aside.

❷ Mince the wood ears and water chestnuts. Squeeze out the excess moisture from both (illus. 1) and set aside.

❸ Preheat 3 tablespoons oil for 2 minutes. Add ① and fry for 2 minutes (illus. 2). Stir in the marinated pork shreds, the minced wood ears, and the minced water chestnuts, blending thoroughly (illus. 3). Heat in the microwave for 2 minutes and 30 seconds. Remove, sprinkle some chopped green onion over the top, and serve.

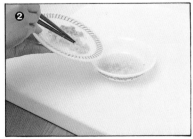

糖醋排骨

Sweet and Sour Ribs

材料：

小排骨	·······	400公克
	水 ·················	6大匙
	番茄醬、白醋···	各3大匙
	糖 ·················	2大匙
①	酒 ·················	1大匙
	太白粉···········	1小匙
	塩 ·················	¼小匙
	味精·············	⅛小匙

❶小排洗淨，剁成12小塊（圖１），入①料醃半小時，再入微波爐加熱20分鐘。中途每隔５分鐘取出翻面一次（圖２）共四次即可。

INGREDIENTS:

400g (14 oz.)		pork ribs
	6 T.	water
	3 T. each:	ketchup, white rice vinegar
	2 T.	sugar
①	1 T.	cooking wine
	1 t.	cornstarch
	¼ t.	salt
	⅛ t.	MSG

❶ Wash the pork ribs and chop into 12 chunks (illus. 1; or have your butcher do it for you). Marinate in ① for half an hour, then heat in the microwave for 20 minutes. Remove from the oven every 5 minutes (a total of four times) to turn the meat over (illus. 2). Serve.

6人份
SERVES 6

义 燒 肉

Cantonese Style Roast Pork

材料：

梅花肉……………… 450公克

① { 味全海鮮醬…… 6大匙
   水……………… 2大匙
   食用紅色素……… 少許

❶ 梅花肉切長條狀（圖1），入①料醃隔夜。
❷ 烤盤預熱6分鐘，放入醃好之梅花肉，以70％電力加熱9分鐘，中途翻面一次即可（圖2）。

INGREDIENTS:

450g (1lb.)   pork, part fat

① { 6 T.   Wei-Chuan brand Hoisin Sauce
   2 T.   water
   few drops red food coloring

❶ Cut the pork into thick, long strips (illus. 1). Marinate in ① overnight.
❷ Preheat a baking dish for 6 minutes in the microwave. Place the marinated pork in the dish, and microwave at 70% power for 9 minutes. Remove halfway through the cooking process to turn the meat over once. (illus. 2) Serve.

6人份
SERVES 6

印度煎排骨

Indian Style Pan-Fried Ribs

材料：

排骨……6塊（約390公克）	油、醬油……各1大匙
洋葱絲……………80公克	咖哩粉、蒜末、糖、
油………………… 2大匙	酒………各½大匙
	① 塩、五香粉…………
	……………各½小匙
	味精、胡椒粉………
	……………各少許

❶排骨切成長條塊狀6塊（圖1），再與洋葱及①料拌勻醃30分鐘。

❷油2大匙入烤盤，預熱4分鐘，依序放入排骨及洋葱（圖2）煎3分鐘，再翻面續熱2分鐘即可。

INGREDIENTS:

390g (14 oz.)		pork ribs
80g (3 oz.)		onion rings, halved
2 T.		cooking oil
①	1 T. each:	cooking oil, soy sauce
	½ T. each:	curry powder, minced garlic, sugar, cooking wine
	½ t. each:	salt, five-spice power
	pinch each of MSG, pepper	

❶ Cut the ribs into long strips (illus. 1). Mix in the onion and ① until blended. Marinate for 30 minutes.

❷ Add 2 tablespoons oil to a baking dish and preheat for 4 minutes. Arrange the ribs and onion in the dish (illus. 2) and fry in the microwave for 3 minutes. Turn over the meat and microwave another 2 minutes. Serve.

6人份
SERVES 6

螞蟻上樹

Ants Climbing a Tree

材料：

絞肉‧‧‧‧‧‧‧‧‧‧‧ 100公克	
粉絲（乾重）‧‧‧‧‧‧‧60公克	
油‧‧‧‧‧‧‧‧‧‧‧‧‧‧ 2大匙	
① { 葱末‧‧‧‧‧‧‧‧‧‧ 2大匙	
辣豆瓣醬‧‧‧‧‧‧¾大匙	
薑末‧‧‧‧‧‧‧‧‧‧½大匙	

② {
水‧‧‧‧‧‧‧‧‧‧‧‧‧‧ 1杯
醬油‧‧‧‧‧‧‧‧‧‧ 1大匙
塩、糖‧‧‧‧‧‧各½小匙
麻油‧‧‧‧‧‧‧‧‧‧‧¼小匙
味精‧‧‧‧‧‧‧‧‧‧‧⅛小匙

❶粉絲用開水泡軟（圖1），切成數段（圖2）備用。
❷油預熱2分鐘，入①料及絞肉加熱1分鐘後，再入
　粉絲及②料加蓋續熱3分鐘即可。

INGREDIENTS:

100g (3½ oz.)	ground pork
60g (2 oz.)	bean thread (dry weight)
2 T.	cooking oil
① { 2 T.	minced green onion
¾ T.	hot bean paste
½ T.	minced ginger root
② { 1 c.	water
1 T.	soy sauce
½ t. each:	salt, sugar
¼ t.	sesame oil
⅛ t.	MSG

❶ Soak the bean thread in hot water until soft
(illus. 1), and cut several times (illus. 2).
❷ Preheat the oil for 2 minutes. Add ① and the
ground pork. Microwave for 1 minute. Add
the soaked bean thread and ②. Cover and
heat another 3 minutes. Serve.

6人份
SERVES 6

三杯鷄 / "Three Cup" Chicken

材料：

雞腿············ 600公克	①	薑············20片	
九層塔嫩葉(圖1)········		蒜(拍碎)········ 2粒	
············20公克	②	醬油、酒······各¼杯	
黑麻油·········· 2大匙		糖············2小匙	

❶ 雞腿洗淨去肥油，剁成3×3公分塊狀(圖2)，置盤，中入微波爐加熱5分鐘，取出洗淨備用，九層塔嫩葉也洗淨備用。

❷ 黑麻油入微波爐預熱2分鐘，爆香①料1分30秒（圖3）後，取出與雞肉及②料拌勻，再入微波爐加熱12分鐘，取出拌入九層塔嫩葉即可。

■ 1. 如無九層塔，可增加薑的份量。

　 2. 黑麻油應選褐紅色，看起來清澄、味香濃者。

"Three Cup" Chicken

INGREDIENTS:

600g (1⅓ lb.)		chicken legs
20g (⅔ to ¾ oz.)		fresh sweet basil leaves (illus. 1)
2 T.		dark sesame oil
①	20 slices	ginger root
	2 cloves	garlic, smashed
②	¼ c. each:	soy sauce, cooking wine
	2 t.	sugar

❶ Wash the chicken legs and remove excess fat. Chop into 3×3 cm (1¼"×1¼") pieces (illus. 2). Place in a baking dish and heat in the microwave for 5 minutes. Remove, wash, and set aside. Choose the freshest and most tender of the basil leaves, wash, and set aside.

❷ Preheat the dark sesame oil in the microwave for 2 minutes. Fry ① in the oil for 1 minute and 30 seconds (illus. 3). Mix in the chicken and ②. Return to the microwave and heat for 12 minutes. Mix in the fresh basil leaves and serve.

■ 1. If fresh basil is unavailable, increase the amount of ginger root used.

　 2. Choose dark sesame oil that is reddish brown, clear, and with a rich aroma.

6人份
SERVES 6

宮保雞丁 | Kung Pao Chicken

材料：

雞胸肉	300公克		醬油	1大匙	
蒜頭花生	40公克		糖	2小匙	
油	3大匙	③	黑醋	1小匙	
① { 乾辣椒	4條		麻油	½小匙	
花椒粒	½小匙		塩、味精	各⅛小匙	
水	3大匙		胡椒粉	少許	
② { 醬油	1大匙				
酒	½大匙				
太白粉	1小匙				
塩	¼小匙				
胡椒粉	⅛小匙				

❶雞肉拍鬆（圖1），切成1公分方塊（圖2），入②料醃約20分鐘備用。

❷乾辣椒剪斜段（圖3），去籽備用。

❸油3大匙預熱2分鐘，再爆香①料2分鐘，隨入醃好的雞丁及③料，拌勻後蓋上保鮮膜續熱5分鐘，取出拌入蒜頭花生即可供食。

INGREDIENTS:

	300g (⅔ lb.)	chicken breast fillets
	40g (1⅓ oz.)	garlic peanuts
	3 T.	cooking oil
① {	4	dried red chili peppers
	½ t.	Szechuan peppercorns
② {	3 T.	water
	1 T.	soy sauce
	½ T.	cooking wine
	1 t.	cornstarch
	¼ t.	salt
	⅛ t.	pepper
③ {	1 T.	soy sauce
	2 t.	sugar
	1 t.	Chinese dark vinegar (Chen chiang tsu)
	½ t.	sesame oil
	⅛ t. each:	salt, MSG
	pinch of pepper	

❶ Pound the chicken breast fillets until tender (illus. 1), then cut into 1cm(½") cubes (illus. 2). Marinate in ② for about 20 minutes. Set aside.

❷ Cut the dried red chili peppers at an angle into medium pieces (illus. 3). Remove seeds and set aside.

❸ Preheat 3 tablespoons oil in a baking dish for two minutes, then fry ① in the oil for another 2 minutes. Finally, add the marinated chicken cubes and ③, blending thoroughly. Cover with plastic wrap and heat in the microwave for 5 minutes. Stir in the peanuts and serve.

紙包鷄

Paper Chicken

材料：

雞胸肉	150公克		水	2大匙
豌豆莢	12片		酒	1大匙
葱絲	¼杯		醬油	½大匙
薑絲	2大匙	①	麻油	1小匙
紅辣椒	1條		塩	¼小匙
玻璃紙			味精	⅛小匙
……12張（約13公分見方）			胡椒粉	少許

❶ 雞胸肉切成12片（圖1），並用刀背拍鬆（圖2），再
　 與①料拌勻醃約20分鐘。
❷ 紅辣椒去籽、切絲備用，豌豆莢去頭尾備用。
❸ 每張玻璃紙包入一片豌豆莢、一片雞肉及葱、薑、
　 紅辣椒絲（圖3），包好後排入盤中加熱3分鐘即可。

INGREDIENTS:

150g (⅓ lb.)		chicken breast fillets
12 slices		Chinese peapods
¼ c.		shredded green onion
2 T.		shredded ginger root
1		small red chili pepper
12 sheets		cellophane
		(about 13cm or 5'' square)
	2 T.	water
	1 T.	cooking wine
①	½ T.	soy sauce
	1 t.	sesame oil
	¼ t.	salt
	⅛ t.	MSG
	pinch of pepper	

❶ Cut the chicken breast fillets into 12 pieces (illus. 1), then pound the pieces tender with the dull edge of a cleaver (illus. 2). Mix in ① and marinate for 20 minutes.

❷ Remove seeds from the red chili pepper, shred, and set aside. Snap off both ends of the Chinese peapods and set aside.

❸ On each sheet of cellophane paper place one peapod, one piece of chicken, and some shredded green onion, ginger root, and red chili pepper (illus. 3). Wrap each one into a small package, arrange on a platter, and heat for 3 minutes in the microwave. Serve.

烤　鷄　腿

Baked Chicken Legs

材料：

大雞腿		3隻（850公克）
①	蒜（切末）	3粒
	薑	3片
	葱段	12段
	醬油	3大匙
	酒	1大匙
	糖、花椒粒	各½大匙
	五香粉	1小匙
	塩	¾小匙

❶ 雞腿內側劃開一刀，入①料醃約半小時，備用。

❷ 烤盤預熱５分鐘，將醃好的雞腿表面向下（圖１）放入已預熱的烤盤上，加熱５分鐘後，翻面（圖２）續熱５分鐘即可。

INGREDIENTS:

3		chicken legs with thighs (850g or 1 lb. 14 oz.)
①	3 cloves	garlic, minced
	3 slices	ginger root
	12 sections (1½'')	green onion
	3 T.	soy sauce
	1 T.	cooking wine
	½ T. each:	sugar, Szechuan peppercorns
	1 t.	Chinese five-spice powder
	¾ t.	salt

❶ Score the chicken at the inner side of the joint between the leg and thigh. Add ① to the chicken and marinate about 30 minutes. Set aside.

❷ Preheat a baking dish for 5 minutes. Place the marinated chicken in the preheated baking dish, outer surface down (illus. 1). Heat 5 minutes in the microwave, then remove to turn over the meat (illus. 2). Heat for another 5 minutes. Serve.

6人份
SERVES 6

醉　　鷄

材料：

	雞…… 半隻（750公克）		紹興酒、高湯………
①	葱段…………………18段	②	………………… 各2杯
	薑………………… 4片		塩……………½小匙
	水………………… 3杯		
	塩………… 1½小匙		

❶雞洗淨入①料加蓋加熱20分鐘，取出雞剁成小塊（圖1），排入碗內（圖2），加②料放入冰箱醃一天以上，食用時倒出汁液，再將雞塊倒扣在盤上即可。

■ 1. 將煮雞的①料待涼後去油，即可當作②料的高湯。
2. 口味較重者可多泡幾天或多加一點塩。

6人份
SERVES 6

Drunken Chicken

INGREDIENTS:

½		chicken (750g or 1⅔ lb.)
①	18 sections (1½")	green onion
	4 slices	ginger root
	3 c.	water
	1½ t.	salt
②	2 c. each:	Shaohsing rice wine (or other rice wine or sherry), soup stock
	½ t.	salt

❶ Wash the chicken. Add ①, cover, and heat 20 minutes in the microwave. Chop the chicken into small chunks (illus. 1) and arrange in a dish (illus. 2). Add ② and marinate in the refrigerator 24 hours or more. To serve, pour off the liquid, and invert the dish onto a serving platter so that the chicken comes out neatly arranged. Serve.

■ 1. After cooking the chicken in ①, let the liquid cool, skim off the fat, and use for the soup stock called for in ②.
2. For a stronger flavor, marinate for a few days instead of one day, or increase the salt.

蘋果鷄捲

Apple Chicken Roll-ups

材料：

雞胸肉‥‥‥‥‥ 200公克	水‥‥‥‥‥‥ 1大匙
蘋果‥‥‥‥‥‥ 1個	淡色醬油、酒‥‥‥‥
白芝麻、油‥‥‥ 各2大匙 ①	‥‥‥‥ 各1小匙
太白粉‥‥‥‥‥‥ 1小匙	塩‥‥‥‥‥‥½小匙
	味精、胡椒粉‥‥‥‥
	‥‥‥‥‥‥各少許

❶ 雞胸肉攤開切12片（圖1），入①料醃20分鐘。

❷ 蘋果去皮切成1×1×5公分條狀12條，並泡水備用。

❸ 雞片攤開，擺上一條蘋果條捲成筒狀，封口處灑些太白粉（圖2），再滾上白芝麻（圖3）備用。

❹ 烤盤入油2大匙預熱4分鐘，排入雞捲，不加蓋加熱2分鐘後，再翻面續熱1分30秒即可。

■ 1. 沒有淡色醬油（生抽），可以普通醬油代替，只是顏色較暗。

2. 蘋果也可以其他水果代替。

INGREDIENTS:

200g (7 oz.)	chicken breast fillets
1	apple
2 T. each:	white sesame seeds, cooking oil
1 t.	cornstarch
① {	1 T. water
	1 t. each: light-colored soy sauce, cooking wine
	½ t. salt
	pinch each of MSG, pepper

❶ Spread out the chicken breast fillets and cut into 12 strips (illus. 1). Mix in ① and marinate 20 minutes.

❷ Peel the apple and cut into twelve 1 × 1 × 5 cm (½″ × ½″ × 2″) strips. Soak in water and set aside.

❸ Spread out the chicken strips. Roll up one piece of apple inside each chicken strip. Seal the edges with a little cornstarch (illus. 2), then roll in white sesame seeds (illus. 3) and set aside.

❹ Preheat 2 tablespoons oil in a baking dish for 4 minutes in the microwave. Arrange the chicken-apple rolls in the baking dish, and heat in the microwave uncovered for 2 minutes. Turn the rolls over and heat for another 1 minute and 30 seconds. Serve.

■ 1. If light-colored soy sauce is unavailable, regular soy sauce may be substituted; however, the color will be darker.

2. Other kinds of fruit may be substituted for the apple.

怪 味 雞

Strange Flavor Chicken

材料：

雞腿…………… 600公克

① 薑……………… 3片
葱段…………… 6段
酒…………… 1大匙

② 醬油………… 3大匙
葱末……… 1½大匙
芝麻醬、糖、醋、辣
油、麻油、薑末、蒜
末………… 各1大匙
花椒粉、鹽…………
………… 各¼小匙
味精………⅛小匙

❶雞腿洗淨，入①料加蓋加熱5分鐘，使其煮熟並去
血水，取出待涼剁塊(圖1)排盤備用。

❷②料調好淋在剁好的雞塊上即可。

■檢查雞腿是否煮熟，可將牙籤戳進雞腿，若沒有血
水流出，則表示已熟(圖2)。

INGREDIENTS:

	600g (1½ lb.)	chicken legs
①	3 slices	ginger root
	6 sections (1½'')	green onion
	1 T.	cooking wine
②	3 T.	soy sauce
	1½ T.	minced green onion
	1 T. each:	sesame paste, sugar, vinegar, chili oil, sesame oil, minced ginger root, minced garlic
	¼ t. each:	ground Szechuan pepper, salt
	⅛ t.	MSG

❶ Wash the chicken legs, add ①, cover, and heat for 5 minutes in the microwave. Remove, wait until cool, and chop into pieces (illus, 1). Set aside.

❷ Mix ② until thoroughly blended. Drizzle over the chicken pieces and serve.

■ To test the chicken legs for doneness, insert a toothpick. They are done if no bloody liquid comes out (illus. 2).

6人份

SERVES 6

沙茶鷄丁

Chicken with Chinese Barbecue Sauce

材料：

雞胸肉··········	350公克
洋葱··········	120公克
油··········	2大匙

	沙茶········	2½大匙
	酒、醬油、水·········	
	·········	各1大匙
①	糖··········	⅔小匙
	塩··········	½小匙
	味精··········	少許

❶雞胸肉洗淨切成２公分丁狀，入①料醃30分鐘，洋葱切塊備用。

❷油２大匙預熱２分鐘，入洋葱塊拌勻（圖１），續熱１分鐘後拌入雞胸肉（圖２），蓋上保鮮膜加熱５分鐘即可。

INGREDIENTS:

350g (¾ lb.)	chicken breast fillets
120g (¼ lb.)	onion
2 T.	cooking oil
2½ T.	Chinese barbecue sauce (sha cha chiang)
1 T. each:	cooking wine, soy sauce, water
① ⅔ t.	sugar
½ t.	salt
pinch of MSG	

❶ Wash the chicken breast fillets and cut into 2 cm (⁴⁄₅'') cubes. Mix in ① and marinate 30 minutes. Cube the onion and set aside.

❷ Preheat 2 tablespoons oil in a baking dish for 2 minutes in the microwave. Mix in the onion (illus. 1) and heat for another minute. Stir in the chicken (illus. 2), cover with plastic wrap, and heat in the microwave for 5 minutes. Serve.

6 人份
SERVES 6

薑味雞腿

Gingered Chicken Legs

材料：
小雞腿…950公克（約6隻）

① 蜂蜜、甜辣醬………
………… 各5大匙
醬油………… 3大匙
薑末………… 1大匙
塩…………½小匙
胡椒粉………¼小匙

② 水………… 2大匙
太白粉………… 1大匙

❶小雞腿洗淨備用，①料拌勻備用。
❷烤盤預熱４分鐘後入雞腿，再淋上①料（圖１），加熱16分鐘，取出雞腿排盤，剩餘汁液拌入②料（圖２），續熱30秒即可淋在雞腿上供食。

INGREDIENTS:

950g (2 lb.)	chicken legs (about 6)
① 5 T. each:	Taiwanese sweet hot sauce, honey
3 T.	soy sauce
1 T.	minced ginger root
½ t.	salt
¼ t.	pepper
② 2 T.	water
1 T.	cornstarch

❶ Wash the chicken legs and set aside. Mix the ingredients in ① together thoroughly.
❷ Preheat a baking dish for 4 minutes in the microwave. Arrange the chicken legs in the dish, drizzle ① over the chicken (illus. 1), and heat in the microwave 16 minutes. Remove the chicken legs from the dish and arrange on a serving platter. Mix ② into the liquid remaining from heating the chicken (illus. 2). Heat for 30 seconds in the microwave, drizzle over the chicken legs, and serve.

6人份
SERVES 6

葱油淋鷄

Chicken with Scallions and Oil

材料：

雞半隻…………	600公克	葱絲…………	50公克
油………………	4大匙	② 嫩薑絲………	30公克
① 酒……………	1大匙	高湯…………	½杯
塩…………	1½小匙		
味精…………	¼小匙		
胡椒粉………	⅛小匙		

❶ 雞洗淨入①料醃約半小時（圖1），蓋上保鮮膜加熱7分鐘，取出待涼後剁塊（圖2），排盤備用。

❷ 油4大匙預熱2分鐘，隨入②料，續熱2分鐘，取出淋在雞塊上即可。

INGREDIENTS:

½	chicken (600g or 1⅓ lb.)
4 T.	cooking oil
① 1 T.	cooking wine
1½ t.	salt
¼ t.	MSG
⅛ t.	pepper
② 50g (1⅔ oz.)	shredded green onion
30g (1 oz.)	shredded young ginger root
½ c.	soup stock

❶ Wash the chicken, and marinate in ① for about half an hour (illus. 1). Cover with plastic wrap and heat 7 minutes in the microwave. Remove and allow to cool. Chop the chicken into chunks (illus. 2) and arrange on a serving platter.

❷ Preheat 4 tablespoons oil in a baking dish for 2 minutes in the microwave. Add ② and heat for another 2 minutes. Remove and drizzle over the chicken. Serve.

6人份
SERVES 6

陳皮牛肉

Beef with Orange Peel

材料：

牛里肌肉········ 300公克	
陳皮·············10公克	

① 　水············· 2大匙
　酒、醬油··· 各1大匙
　糖、太白粉··········
　············· 各1小匙
　塩·············½小匙
　味精·········⅛小匙

② 　乾辣椒········ 4公克
　八角············· 1朶
　油············· 3大匙
　花椒粒·······¼小匙

❶牛肉洗淨切片，陳皮切與牛肉同等大小片狀，一起
與①料拌勻，醃約20分鐘備用。
❷爆香②料4分鐘（圖1），再拌入醃好的牛肉片（圖
2），蓋上保鮮膜後續熱2分鐘即可。

INGREDIENTS:

300g (⅔ lb.)		lean beef
10g (⅓ to ½ oz.)		dried orange or tangerine peel
①	2 T.	water
	1 T. each:	cooking wine, soy sauce
	1 t. each:	sugar, cornstarch
	½ t.	salt
	⅛ t.	MSG
②	4 g (⅕ oz.)	dried red chili pepper
	1 floweret	star anise
	3 T.	cooking oil
	¼ t.	Szechuan peppercorns

❶ Wash the beef and slice thinly. Cut the dried orange peel into pieces about the same size as the beef slices, and marinate the two together in ① for about 20 minutes. Set aside.

❷ Fry ② for 4 minutes in the microwave (illus. 1), then mix in the marinated beef and orange peel (illus. 2). Cover with plastic wrap and heat for another 2 minutes in the microwave. Serve.

6人份
SERVES 6

葱爆牛肉

Flash-Fried Beef with Scallions

材料：

牛里肌肉········ 300公克	①	油·············· 2大匙
葱··············· 100公克		醬油··········· 2小匙
油··················· 2大匙		酒、玉米粉·各1小匙
		糖、塩······各¼小匙
		小蘇打········⅛小匙
		麻油·············少許

❶牛肉切片入①料醃約20分鐘備用。
❷葱洗淨，去老葉（圖1），切段（圖2）備用。
❸油2大匙預熱3分鐘後，爆香葱段3分鐘，再拌入
醃好的牛肉片，蓋上保鮮膜後續熱2分30秒即可。

INGREDIENTS:

300g (⅔ lb.)	lean beef
100g (3½ oz.)	green onion
2 T.	cooking oil
①	2 T.	cooking oil
	2 t.	soy sauce
	1 t. each:	cooking wine, cornstarch
	¼ t. each:	sugar, salt
	⅛ t.	baking soda
	dash of sesame oil

❶ Slice the beef thinly, and marinate in ① for
about 20 minutes. Set aside.
❷ Wash the green onion, remove any wilted and
tough leaves (illus. 1), and cut at an angle into
4 cm (1½'') lengths (illus. 2). Set aside.
❸ Preheat 2 tablespoons oil in the microwave for
3 minutes, then fry the cut green onion in the
oil for another 3 minutes. Mix in the marinated
beef slices and cover with plastic wrap. Cook
for 2 minutes and 30 seconds. Serve.

6人份
SERVES 6

家常牛肉絲

Home Style Shredded Beef

材料：

牛里肌肉	220公克	醬油、酒… 各1小匙	
芹菜（淨重）	110公克	辣豆瓣醬、黑醋……	②
紅辣椒	半條	各1小匙	
嫩薑	6片	塩、糖……各¼小匙	
水	6大匙	味精……⅛小匙	
油	2大匙		
① 醬油	1大匙		
太白粉	1小匙		
小蘇打	¼小匙		

❶牛肉切細絲（圖1），入①料醃約10分鐘備用。

❷芹菜去根葉洗淨（淨重為110公克），切成4公分長段
（圖2）備用，紅辣椒去籽切絲，薑片切細絲備用。

❸將醃好的牛肉平鋪盤中（圖3），蓋上保鮮膜後加熱
3分鐘，取出拌入芹菜、紅辣椒絲、薑絲及②料，
加蓋後續熱2分鐘即可。

INGREDIENTS:

220g. (½ lb.)		lean beef
110g. (¼ lb.)		celery (net weight)
½		red chili pepper
6 slices		young ginger root
①	6 T.	water
	2 T.	cooking oil
	1 T.	soy sauce
	1 t.	cornstarch
	¼ t.	baking soda
②	1 t. each:	soy sauce, cooking wine
	1 t. each:	hot bean paste, Chinese dark vinegar
	¼ t. each:	salt, sugar
	⅛ t.	MSG

❶ Shred the beef (illus. 1). Marinate in ① for about 10 minutes. Set aside.

❷ Cut off the leaves and root portion from the celery, wash, and cut into 4 cm (1½'') pieces (illus. 2). Set aside. Remove the seeds from the red chili pepper and shred. Shred the young ginger root slices. Set aside.

❸ Spread the marinated beef evenly over a baking dish (illus. 3). Cover with plastic wrap and heat in the microwave for 3 minutes. Remove and mix in the celery, red chili pepper, shredded ginger, and ②. Cover, heat another 2 minutes, and serve.

黑椒牛柳

Black Pepper Steak

材料：

牛里肌肉·········	300公克
洋葱(淨重)······	150公克
油·················	2大匙

① 水················· 6大匙
醬油············· 2大匙
油、太白粉·········
············· 各1大匙
塩············· ¼小匙

② 水················· 1大匙
蠔油、黑胡椒·········
············· 各1小匙
塩、糖、味精·········
············· 各⅛小匙

❶牛肉切成6×0.5×0.5公分長條，入①料醃約1½小時備用，洋葱切絲備用。

❷洋葱絲加油2大匙(圖1)，拌勻置盤中，蓋上保鮮膜加熱4分鐘後，續入牛肉條(圖2)及②料，拌勻續熱2分鐘即可。

如喜愛黑胡椒味道者，可酌量增加份量。

INGREDIENTS:

300g (⅔ lb.)	lean beef
150g. (⅓ lb.)	onion (net weight)
2 T.	cooking oil

① 6 T. water
2 T. soy sauce
1 T. each: cooking oil, cornstarch
¼ t. salt

② 1 T. water
1 t. each: oyster sauce, black pepper
⅛ t. each: salt, sugar, MSG

❶ Cut the beef into 6×0.5×0.5 cm (2½'' × ¼'' × ¼'') strips. Marinate in ① for about 1½ hours. Cut the onion into half-rings. Set aside.

❷ Add 2 tablespoons oil to the onions (illus. 1) and place in a baking dish. Cover with plastic wrap and heat in the microwave for 4 minutes. Add the beef (illus. 2) and ②, mix well, heat for another 2 minutes, and serve.

■ Those who like a more peppery steak can increase the amount of black pepper used.

6人份
SERVES 6

青椒牛肉絲

Shredded Beef with Green Pepper

材料：

| 牛肉‥‥‥‥‥ 220公克 | ② | 塩‥‥‥‥‥¼小匙 |
| 青椒‥‥‥‥‥ 200公克 | | 味精‥‥‥‥⅛小匙 |

① ⎰ 水‥‥‥‥‥ 4大匙
⎪ 油‥‥‥‥‥ 2大匙
⎪ 醬油‥‥‥‥ 1大匙
⎨ 酒‥‥‥‥‥ ½大匙
⎪ 太白粉‥‥‥ 2小匙
⎩ 塩‥‥‥‥‥ ½小匙

❶牛肉逆紋切細絲（圖１）後，入①料醃約10分鐘備用。
❷青椒去籽（圖２）洗淨，切絲備用。
❸醃好的牛肉置盤中，蓋上保鮮膜加熱２分30秒，取出拌入②料及青椒絲，續熱１分30秒即可。

INGREDIENTS:

| 220g (½ lb.) | beef |
| 200g (7 oz.) | green pepper |

① ⎰ 4 T. | water
⎪ 2 T. | cooking oil
⎪ 1 T. | soy sauce
⎨ ½ T. | cooking wine
⎪ 2 t. | cornstarch
⎩ ½ t. | salt

② ⎰ ¼ t. | salt
⎩ ⅛ t. | MSG

❶ Shred the beef against the grain (illus. 1). Marinate in ① for about 10 minutes. Set aside.
❷ Remove the seeds from the green pepper (illus. 2), wash, and cut into julienne strips. Set aside.
❸ Spread the marinated shredded beef in a baking dish, cover with plastic wrap, and heat in the microwave for 2 minutes and 30 seconds. Remove, mix in ② and the green peppers, and heat for another minute and 30 seconds. Serve.

6人份
SERVES 6

沙茶牛肉

Beef with Chinese Barbecue Sauce

材料：

牛里肌肉········ 300公克		水·············· 4大匙
洋葱(淨重)····· 100公克		沙茶醬······· 2大匙
油················· 2大匙	①	醬油······· 1½大匙
		油、酒····· 各1大匙
		糖·············⅔小匙
		小蘇打········⅛小匙

❶牛肉切薄片，入①料醃約30分鐘，洋葱切2.5×2.5公分塊狀備用。

❷油2大匙預熱2分鐘後，爆香洋葱塊2分鐘(圖1)，續入醃好的牛肉片(圖2)，加熱3分鐘即可。

INGREDIENTS:

300g (⅔ lb.)		lean beef
100g (3½ oz.)		onion (net weight)
2 T.		cooking oil
	4 T.	water
	2 T.	Chinese barbecue sauce (sha cha chiang)
①	1½ T.	soy sauce
	1 T. each:	cooking oil, cooking wine
	⅔ t.	sugar
	⅛ t.	baking soda

❶ Cut the beef into thin slices and marinate in ① for about half an hour. Cut the onion into 2.5 cm (1'') cubes. Set aside.

❷ Preheat 2 tablespoons oil for 2 minutes in the microwave. Fry the onion in the oil for another 2 minutes (illus. 1), then add the marinated beef slices (illus. 2) and heat for another 3 minutes. Serve.

6人份
SERVES 6

薑絲牛肉

Ginger Beef

材料：

牛肉·············· 300公克	
嫩薑絲··············50公克	
油·················· 3大匙	

① 醬油、蠔油、水、酒
·············· 各1大匙
麻油··········½小匙
糖············¼小匙
味精、胡椒粉·······
··············各少許

❶牛肉切絲，入①料醃約15分鐘備用。

❷油３大匙預熱２分鐘，爆香嫩薑絲(圖１)１分30秒
後，入醃好的牛肉絲(圖２)，並拌勻續熱２分30秒
即可。

INGREDIENTS:

300g (⅔ lb.)	beef
50g (1¾ oz.)	shredded young ginger root
3 T.	cooking oil

① 1 T. each: soy sauce, oyster sauce, water, cooking wine
½ t. sesame oil
¼ t. sugar
pinch each of MSG, pepper

❶ Shred the beef and marinate in ① for about 15 minutes. Set aside.

❷ Preheat 3 tablespoons oil for 2 minutes in the microwave. Fry the shredded young ginger in the oil (illus. 1) for 1 minute and 30 seconds. Add the marinated beef (illus. 2), mixing well. Heat 2 minutes and 30 seconds, and serve.

蘆筍蝦捲

Shrimp-Asparagus Rolls

材料：

蝦仁…………… 200公克	
綠蘆筍…………90公克	
肥肉…………… 20公克 ①	葱末、薑末、太白粉 …………… 各1小匙 塩…………¼小匙 味精………⅛小匙 麻油、胡椒粉……… …………各少許

❶ 綠蘆筍切成10公分長段12段備用。

❷ 蝦仁洗淨，抽去沙腸與肥肉一起剁成泥狀(圖1)，入①料調成蝦泥後甩打數下，使有彈性，再分成12等份備用。

❸ 每份蝦泥先壓成皮狀(圖2)，再包住蘆筍(圖3)，讓頭尾稍露出一點，不要全部包滿，如此依序做完12份。

❹ 烤盤入油2大匙預熱4分鐘，排入蘆筍蝦捲，加熱2分鐘後，翻面續熱1分30秒即可。

INGREDIENTS:

200g (7 oz.)	shelled shrimp
90g (3 oz.)	fresh green asparagus
20g (¾ oz.)	fat pork
①	1 t. each: minced green onion, minced ginger root, cornstarch ¼ t. salt ⅛ t. MSG dash of sesame oil pinch of pepper

❶ Cut the asparagus into twelve 10cm(4'') sections. Set aside.

❷ Wash the shrimp, devein, and chop into a paste together with the pork (illus. 1). Mix in ①, then roll the mixture into a ball and throw against a cutting board several times (this gives it a springier texture). Divide the mixture into 12 equal portions and set aside.

❸ Flatten out each portion of the shrimp mixture (illus. 2), then wrap around the fresh asparagus (illus. 3). Allow the ends to protrude a little. Repeat until all ingredients are used up.

❹ Place 2 tablespoons cooking oil in a baking dish and preheat for 4 minutes in the microwave. Arrange the shrimp-asparagus rolls in the dish and return to the microwave for another 2 minutes. Turn over and heat for another minute and 30 seconds. Serve.

6人份

茄汁大蝦 / Shrimp in Tomato Sauce

材料：
草蝦… 300公克（約12尾）

① {
薑……………………… 2片
葱段……………………… 6段
酒……………………… 1大匙
塩……………………… ¼小匙
}

② {
水……………………… ¼杯
番茄醬、糖、醋、油
　　　　　　　各2大匙
塩……………………… ¼小匙
味精……………………… ⅛小匙
}

③ {
水……………………… 1小匙
太白粉……………… ¾小匙
}

❶草蝦剪去鬚脚，並將背部剪開，去腸泥（圖1）洗淨，入①料拌醃10分鐘（圖2），放入盤中加蓋後加熱3分30秒，取出草蝦排盤（圖3）備用。

❷②料放入碗內拌勻，加熱2分鐘，拌入③料勾芡續熱30秒，取出淋在排好的草蝦上即可。

INGREDIENTS:

300g (⅔ lb.)		unshelled shrimp (about 12)
①	2 slices	ginger root
	6 sections (1½")	green onion
	1 T.	cooking wine
	¼ t.	salt
②	¼ c.	water
	2 T. each:	ketchup, sugar, vinegar, cooking oil
	¼ t.	salt
	⅛ t.	MSG
③	1 t.	water
	¾ t.	cornstarch

❶ Clip the feet and antennae off the shrimp. Slit down the back and devein (illus. 1). Wash. Mix in ① and marinate 10 minutes (illus. 2). Arrange in a baking dish, cover, and heat in the microwave for 3 minutes and 30 seconds. Transfer the shrimp to a serving platter (illus. 3) and set aside.

❷ Mix ② together well and heat 2 minutes in the microwave. Mix in ③ and heat in the microwave 30 seconds to thicken. Remove, pour over the top of the shrimp, and serve.

生煎龍鳳捲

Dragon and Phoenix Rolls

材料：

大蝦仁………………………	酒………… 1大匙
……… 24尾（約150公克）①	塩………… ¼小匙
麵包粉……………………¾杯	胡椒粉……… ⅛小匙
太白粉……………………¼杯	
蛋………………………… 1個	
牙籤………………………12枝	
油……………………… 3大匙	

❶蝦仁去腸泥後洗淨，再瀝乾水份入①料醃約10分鐘備用；蛋打散備用。

❷將醃好的蝦仁每兩尾用一枝牙籤串成龍鳳捲（圖1），再依次沾上太白粉、蛋汁及麵包粉（圖2），共12串備用。

❸烤盤入1½大匙油預熱5分鐘，排入6串龍鳳捲加熱1分鐘，翻面（圖3）續熱1分鐘，即可取出排盤。

❹烤盤再入1½大匙油續熱2分鐘，再排入剩餘的6串龍鳳捲，每面各加熱1分鐘即可取出排盤。

■食用時可沾番茄醬，更美味。

INGREDIENTS:

24	large srimp, shelled (about 150g or ⅓ lb.)
¾ c.	fine bread crumbs
¼ c.	cornstarch
1	egg
12	toothpicks
3 T.	cooking oil
① { 1 T.	cooking wine
¼ t.	salt
⅛ t.	pepper

❶ Devein, wash, and drain the shrimp. Mix in ① and marinate 10 minutes. Set aside. Beat the egg lightly and set aside.

❷ Skewer the shrimp, two per toothpick, into 12 dragon and phoenix rolls (illus. 1). Dip each first in the cornstarch, then the beaten egg, and finally the fine bread-crumbs (illus. 2). Set aside.

❸ Preheat 1½ tablespoons cooking oil in a baking dish for 5 minutes in the micro-wave. Arrange 6 of the dragon and phoenix rolls in the dish and heat 1 minute. Turn the shrimp over (illus. 3) and heat another minute. Transfer to a serving platter.

❹ Put another 1½ tablespoons cooking oil in the baking dish and heat 2 minutes. Arrange the remaining 6 Dragon and Phoenix Rolls in the dish, and heat one minute on each side. Transfer to the serving platter and serve.

■ Ketchup may be served as a dip for the Dragon and Phoenix Rolls.

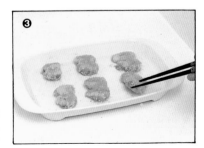

客家生蠔

Oysters Hakka Style

材料：

生蠔（淨重）‧‧‧‧‧‧ 400公克	醬油‧‧‧‧‧‧‧ 1½大匙
九層塔葉‧‧‧‧‧‧‧‧‧‧‧15公克	葱末、水‧‧‧ 各1大匙
酒‧‧‧‧‧‧‧‧‧‧‧‧‧‧‧‧‧‧ 1大匙	蒜末‧‧‧‧‧‧‧‧‧½大匙
	① 紅辣椒末‧‧‧‧‧ 1小匙
	麻油‧‧‧‧‧‧‧‧‧‧½小匙
	塩‧‧‧‧‧‧‧‧‧‧‧‧‧⅓小匙
	味精‧‧‧‧‧‧‧‧‧‧¼小匙
	②太白粉、水‧‧‧ 各1大匙

❶生蠔加酒入微波爐加熱２分30秒，瀝乾水份備用。
❷生蠔加①料，蓋上保鮮膜（圖１）加熱２分鐘後入②
料續熱30秒，再取出趁熱拌入九層塔（圖２）即可。

INGREDIENTS:

400g (14 oz.)		fresh oysters (net weight)
15g (½ oz.)		fresh sweet basil leaves
1 T.		cooking wine
	1½ T.	soy sauce
	1 T. each:	minced green onion, water
①	½ T.	minced garlic
	1 t.	minced red chili pepper
	½ t.	sesame oil
	⅓ t.	salt
	¼ t.	MSG
②	1 T. each:	cornstarch, water

❶ Add the cooking wine to the fresh oysters and heat in the microwave for 2 minutes and 30 seconds. Drain and set aside.
❷ Mix ① and add to the oysters. Cover with plastic wrap (illus. 1) and heat for 2 minutes in the microwave. Add ② and heat for another 30 seconds. Remove, stir in the basil leaves while still hot (illus. 2), and serve.

6人份
SERVES 6

培根生蠔

Bacon-Oyster Wraps

材料：
培根‥‥‥‥‥‥‥‥‥‥六片
大生蠔‥‥‥ 200公克（約18顆）
牙籤‥‥‥‥‥‥‥‥‥‥18枝
酒‥‥‥‥‥‥‥‥‥‥ 1小匙

❶每片培根切成三等分（圖1），備用。
❷生蠔洗淨瀝乾水份，拌入酒，每個生蠔用一片培根
　包起來（圖2）並用牙籤固定，排在盤上，入微波爐
　加熱5分鐘即取出。

INGREDIENTS:

6 slices	bacon
200g (7 oz.)	large fresh oysters (about 18)
18	toothpicks
1 t.	cooking wine

❶ Cut each slice of bacon into three equal portions (illus. 1). Set aside.
❷ Wash and drain the oysters. Mix in the cooking wine. Wrap each oyster in a piece of bacon (illus. 2) and secure with a toothpick. Arrange in a baking dish and heat in the microwave for 5 minutes. Serve.

6人份
SERVES 6

雪菜黃魚

材料：

黃魚一尾…………………
………（淨重）400公克
雪菜……………70公克
紅辣椒末（去籽）…½大匙
① 酒……………1大匙
塩……………¾小匙
胡椒粉………⅛小匙

② 水…………… 3大匙
熟油、淡色醬油……
………… 各2大匙
糖……………¼小匙

❶黃魚洗淨，魚身斜劃二刀（圖1），入①料醃20分鐘，備用。

❷雪菜洗淨切末（圖2）置魚上，灑上紅辣椒末及②料（圖3），蓋上保鮮膜後加熱7分鐘即可。

■在國外買不到雪菜時，可在超級市場買芥菜葉（mustard green），以塩醃2天後即成雪菜。

INGREDIENTS:

1 whole	Chinese yellow croaker (or other white-fleshed fish, 400g or 14 oz. net weight)
70g (2½ oz.)	Chinese salt rape greens
½ T.	minced red chili pepper, seeds removed
① 1 T.	cooking wine
¾ t.	salt
⅛ t.	pepper
② 3 T.	water
2 T. each:	heated and cooled cooking oil, light-colored soy sauce
¼ t.	sugar

❶ Wash the fish. Make two diagonal slashes in the fish (illus. 1). Marinate in ① for 20 minutes. Set aside.

❷ Wash the salt rape greens and mince (illus. 2). Spread over the top of the fish, then sprinkle the minced red chili pepper and ② over the fish (illus. 3), and cover with plastic wrap. Heat for 7 minutes in the microwave and serve.

■ If Chinese salt rape greens are unavailable in your area, you can purchase fresh mustard greens at the supermarket and cure in salt for two days to make your own salted greens.

香菇蒸石斑

材料：

石斑魚…	一尾（750公克）	酒…………… 2小匙	
五花肉…………	40公克 ①	塩…………… ¾小匙	①
香菇…………	6朵	胡椒粉……… ¼小匙	
薑…………	6片	淡色醬油、熟油……	
葱段…………	6段 ②	各2大匙	②
		糖………… ¼小匙	

❶香菇泡軟去蒂，五花肉去皮切薄片備用。

❷石斑魚洗淨，兩面每隔四公分切斜刀深觸及骨（圖1），再入①料醃10分鐘，正面刀口處夾入五花肉片、薑片、葱段及香菇（圖2），底部用筷子架起（圖3），淋上②料，蓋上保鮮膜入微波爐加熱10分鐘即可。

INGREDIENTS:

1 whole	grouper (or other white-fleshed fish; 750g or 1⅔ lb.)
40g (1⅓ oz.)	pork, part lean, part fat
6	dried Chinese black mushrooms
6 slices	ginger root
6 sections (1½")	green onion
① 2 t.	cooking wine
¾ t.	salt
¼ t.	pepper
② 2 T. each:	light-colored soy sauce, heated and cooled cooking oil
¼ t.	sugar

❶ Soak the mushrooms until soft and remove the stems. Remove the rind from the pork (if any) and cut the meat into thin slices. Set aside.

❷ Wash the fish. On both sides of the fish, make diagonal slashes down to the bone at 4 cm (1½") intervals (illus. 1). Marinate in ① for 10 minutes. Insert a pork slice, ginger root slice, green onion section, and a mushroom in each of the slashes on the top side (illus. 2). Place the fish on a plate and then on top of a support made of chopsticks (illus. 3). Sprinkle ② over the top, cover with plastic wrap, and heat in the microwave for 10 minutes. Serve.

蹄筋海參

材料：

- 刺參…………… 300公克
- 蹄筋…………… 150公克
- ①
  - 水………………… 2杯
  - 葱段…………… 6段
  - 薑………………… 4片
  - 酒…………… 1大匙
- ②
  - 油…………… 2大匙
  - 薑末……… 1½大匙
- ③
  - 水…………… 1½杯
  - 醬油………… 2小匙
  - 糖……………¾大匙
  - 酒……………½大匙
  - 塩………… 1¼小匙
  - 麻油………… 1小匙
  - 胡椒粉………⅛小匙
- ④
  - 太白粉、水………… 各1½大匙
- 黑醋…………… 2½大匙

❶刺參、蹄筋洗淨切３公分長段(圖３)，加①料入微波爐加熱４分鐘，取出洗淨瀝乾水份備用。

❷②料入微波爐加熱２分鐘後，入刺參、蹄筋及③料，加蓋加熱６分鐘，取出拌入④料，續熱30秒勾芡，食用前淋上黑醋即可。

■ 海參用清水煮開後(圖１)，即熄火燜之。一天煮２次，約需５至６天脹起後即可(若要快些則稍脹後即可把肚子剪開(圖２)再泡煮。)

Pork Tendons with Sea Cucumber

INGREDIENTS:

	300g (⅔ lb.)	sea cucumber
	150g (⅓ lb.)	pig's feet tendons
①	2 c.	water
	6 sections (1½")	green onion
	4 slices	ginger root
	1 T.	cooking wine
②	2 T.	cooking oil
	1½ T.	minced ginger root
③	1½ c.	water
	2 t.	soy sauce
	¾ T.	sugar
	½ T.	cooking wine
	1¼ t.	salt
	1 t.	sesame oil
	⅛ t.	pepper
④	1½ T. each:	cornstarch, water
	2½ T.	Chinese black vinegar

❶ Wash the sea cucumber and the pork tendons. Cut into 3 cm (1⅕") pieces (illus. 3). Add ① and heat in the microwave for 4 minutes. Remove, wash and drain. Set aside.

❷ Mix ② and heat in the microwave for 2 minutes. Add the sea cucumber, pork tendons, and ③. Cover and heat for 6 minutes. Remove and mix in ④, and heat for another 30 seconds to thicken. Sprinkle on some Chinese black vinegar just before serving.

■ If using dried sea cucumber: place the sea cucumber in a saucepan filled with water and bring to a boil (illus. 1). After the water has begun to boil, turn off the heat and cover. Do this twice a day for 5 to 6 days to reconstitute the dried sea cucumber to its original fullness. (If you are in a hurry, wait until the sea cucumber has partially softened and expanded, then cut it open at the abdomen (illus. 2), and proceed with the boiling and soaking.)

辣醬豆腐

Bean Curd with Hot Sauce

材料：

嫩豆腐	3塊		
青蒜	1枝	水	½杯
油	2大匙	① { 塩	½小匙
辣豆瓣醬	1½大匙	糖	¼小匙
		味精	⅛小匙
		② { 水	1½小匙
		太白粉	1小匙

❶ 嫩豆腐切0.5公分方塊（圖1）置盤，青蒜洗淨切斜片（圖2）備用。

❷ 油2大匙入微波爐預熱2分鐘，爆香辣豆瓣醬1分鐘，取出與①料拌勻，淋在豆腐上（圖3），一起入微波爐加熱5分鐘，取出再拌入②料及青蒜，續熱1分鐘即可。

■ 1. 嫩豆腐即組織較細的豆腐，一般豆腐較硬，煮湯較適宜。

　 2. 在國外買不到青蒜時，可用蒜頭切片代替。

INGREDIENTS:

3 cakes		soft bean curd (tofu)
1		garlic sprout
2 T.		cooking oil
1½ T.		hot bean paste
①	½ c.	water
	½ t.	salt
	¼ t.	sugar
	⅛ t.	MSG
②	1½ t.	water
	1 t.	cornstarch

❶ Cut the bean curd into ¼'' (0.5 cm) cubes (illus. 1) and place in a dish. Wash the garlic sprout, cut into pieces at an angle (illus. 2), and set aside.

❷ Preheat 2 tablespoons oil in the microwave for 2 minutes, then fry the hot bean paste in the oil for 1 minute. Mix with ① until blended, and pour over the bean curd (illus. 3). Heat in the microwave 5 minutes. Stir in ② and the cut garlic sprout. Heat 1 minute and serve.

■ 1. Soft bean curd is light and finely textured; firm bean curd is a good choice when making soup.

　 2. If garlic sprouts are unavailable in your area, use sliced garlic as a substitute.

6 人份
SERVES 6

鑲豆腐　Stuffed Bean Curd

材料：

嫩豆腐	2塊	高湯	½杯
絞肉	75公克	② 醬油	1大匙
蝦仁	30公克	糖、塩	各½小匙

① 太白粉、麻油 各1小匙
葱末 ½小匙
塩、薑末 各¼小匙
糖 ⅛小匙

③ 太白粉、水 各1小匙

❶蝦仁去腸泥洗淨，瀝乾切丁備用。

❷絞肉、蝦仁丁及①料拌勻，甩打數次，再分成12等份蝦泥備用。

❸嫩豆腐切成12份，每份約3×4公分，每個豆腐中央用小湯匙挖一個洞（圖1）鑲入一份蝦泥（圖2）。鑲完12個豆腐後，排入深盤內，淋上②料（圖3），加蓋加熱8分鐘，取出，並將汁液倒在小碗內備用。

❹③料與小碗內之汁液拌勻，入微波爐勾芡加熱30秒，取出淋在鑲豆腐上即可。

INGREDIENTS:

	2 cakes	soft bean curd
	75g (2½ oz.)	ground pork
	30g (1 oz.)	shelled shrimp
①	1 t. each:	cornstarch, sesame oil
	½ t.	minced green onion
	¼ t. each:	salt, minced ginger root
	⅛ t.	sugar
②	½ c.	soup stock
	1 T.	soy sauce
	½ t. each:	sugar, salt
③	1 t. each:	cornstarch, water

❶ Devein the shrimp, wash, drain, and cut into cubes. Set aside.

❷ Mix the ground pork, shrimp, and ① together thoroughly. Throw against a counter or cutting board several times (this improves the texture). Divide into 12 equal portions and set aside.

❸ Cut the bean curd into 12 squares, each about 3 × 4 cm (1¼″ × 1⅔″). With a small spoon, scoop out a hole in each piece of bean curd (illus. 1). Stuff with the ground pork-shrimp paste (illus. 2). After stuffing all the pieces of bean curd, arrange on a platter and sprinkle ② over the top (illus. 3). Cover and heat 8 minutes in the microwave. Pour the liquid off into a small bowl after cooking.

❹ Mix ③ into the liquid in the small bowl and heat 30 seconds in the microwave to thicken. Pour over the stuffed bean curd and serve.

白玉鮑脯　　　　White Jade Abalone

材料：

嫩豆腐	3塊
鮑魚	60公克
絞肉	50公克
水	4杯
高湯	3杯
沙拉油	1大匙

① 淡色醬油 …… ½小匙
　 酒 …………… ¼小匙
　 蒜片 ………… 4片
　 薑片 ………… 2片

② 沙拉油 ……… 2小匙
　 酒、太白粉、麵粉…
　 ………… 各1小匙
　 塩 …………… ½小匙
　 胡椒粉 ……… ¼小匙
　 蛋白 ………… 2個

③ 高湯 …………… ¾杯
　 塩 …………… ⅛小匙

④ 太白粉、水…
　 ………… 各1小匙

❶ 絞肉以①料醃10分鐘取出蒜、薑片，隨入 1 大匙沙拉油拌勻，爆香絞肉50秒取出備用。

❷ 鮑魚切片直舖于扣碗上（圖 1 ）備用。

❸ 豆腐加水 4 杯蓋上保鮮膜，加熱10分鐘後倒出水份，入高湯續熱10分鐘，取出豆腐加入爆香之絞肉及②料，搗碎並拌勻（圖 2 ）倒入扣碗中（圖 3 ），再蓋上保鮮膜加熱 7 分鐘，取出倒扣于盤上即爲鮑脯。

❹ ③料加熱 1 分30秒，入④料略拌續熱30秒後取出，淋于盤內鮑脯即成。

INGREDIENTS:

3 cakes	soft bean curd
60g (2 oz.)	abalone
50g (1¾ oz.)	ground pork
4 c.	water
3 c.	soup stock
1 T.	cooking oil

① ½ t. — light-colored soy sauce
　 ¼ t. — cooking wine
　 4 slices — garlic
　 2 slices — ginger root

② 2 t. — cooking oil
　 1 t. each: — wine, cornstarch, flour
　 ½ t. — salt
　 ¼ t. — pepper
　 2 — egg whites

③ ¾ c. — soup stock
　 ⅛ t. — salt

④ 1 t. — cornstarch
　 1 t. — water

❶ Marinate the ground pork in ① for 10 minutes. Remove the garlic and ginger root slices, and stir in 1 tablespoon oil. Fry the pork 50 seconds in the microwave. Set aside.

❷ Cut the abalone into slices and arrange inside a bowl (illus. 1). Set aside.

❸ Add 4 cups water to the bean curd, cover with plastic wrap, and heat in the microwave 10 minutes. Pour off the water, pour in the soup stock, and heat 10 minutes. Add the ground pork and ② to the bean card. Break apart the ground pork and bean curd, mixing the ingredients until well blended (illus. 2). Transfer to the abalone-lined bowl (illus. 3). Cover with plastic wrap and heat 7 minutes in the microwave. Invert on a serving plate.

❹ Heat ③ 1 minute and 30 seconds, then mix in ④ and heat 30 seconds. Pour over the abalone and bean curd and serve.

香菇素腸

Vegetarian Sausage with Mushrooms

材料：

素腸·············· 300公克		水················¼杯	
香菇······ 30公克（約9朵）		醬油··········· 3大匙	
薑絲···············20公克	①	麻油··········· 1小匙	
油·················· 2大匙		塩···············⅛小匙	
		胡椒粉··········少許	

❶香菇泡軟去蒂切絲，素腸洗淨用手撕成絲狀（圖1）備用。

❷油2大匙預熱2分鐘，爆香香菇及薑絲2分鐘，入素腸絲及①料並拌勻（圖2），蓋上保鮮膜續熱3分鐘即可。

INGREDIENTS:

300g (⅔ lb.)	vegetarian (bean curd) sausage
30g (1 oz.)	dried Chinese black mushrooms (about 9)
20g (⅔ oz.)	shredded ginger
2 T.	cooking oil

	¼ c.	water
	3 T.	soy sauce
①	1 t.	sesame oil
	⅛ t.	salt
	pinch of pepper	

❶ Soak the mushrooms until soft, remove the stems, and cut into julienne strips. Wash the vegetarian sausage and tear into shreds (illus. 1). Set aside.

❷ Preheat 2 tablespoons oil for 2 minutes in the microwave. Fry the mushroom and shredded ginger root 2 minutes. Add the shredded vegetarian sausage and ① and mix well (illus. 2). Cover with plastic wrap, heat 3 minutes, and serve.

6人份
SERVES 6

蛤蜊蒸蛋

Steamed Egg with Clams

材料：

大蛤蜊……180公克（6個）		熱水…	2杯（約75℃）
雞蛋……………… 3個		油……………	½大匙
魚板…………60公克	①	塩……………	¾小匙
葱末……………少許		糖、酒……各¼小匙
		味精…………	⅛小匙

❶蛤蜊吐沙（圖１），２小時後洗淨，置盤並加蓋入微波爐加熱１分30秒備用。

❷魚板切絲（圖２）備用。

❸蛋打散入❶料、魚板絲及①料加蓋入微波爐以60％電力加熱10分鐘，取出灑上葱花即可。

INGREDIENTS:

180g (6½ oz.)		large clams (6)
3		eggs
60g (2 oz.)		fish cake
minced green onion, as desired		
	2 c.	hot water (about 170°F or 75°C)
	½ T.	cooking oil
①	¾ t.	salt
	¼ t. each:	sugar, cooking wine
	⅛ t.	MSG

❶ Allow the clams to expel the sand they contain by soaking in water for 2 hours (illus. 1). Wash, place in a dish, cover, and heat in the microwave 1 minute and 30 seconds. Set aside.

❷ Cut the fish cake into thin strips (illus. 2) and set aside.

❸ Beat the egg lightly and mix in ①, the fish cake, and the clams. Cover and heat 10 minutes in the microwave at 60% power. Sprinkle chopped green onion over the top and serve.

6 人份
SERVES 6

芙蓉蛋

Egg Foo Yung

材料：

蛋	5個	②	高湯	½杯
蝦仁	120公克		太白粉	½小匙
葱末	3大匙		醬油	¼小匙
① 油	1大匙		塩、味精	各少許
塩	¼小匙			

❶蝦仁去腸泥，洗淨，瀝乾水份備用，蛋打散備用。

❷蛋液和①料拌勻（圖1），入微波爐以70％的電力加熱2分鐘，取出（圖2）備用。

❸蝦仁、葱末與❷料拌勻（圖3），續入微波爐以70％的電力加熱5分鐘。

❹②料拌勻加熱2分鐘，取出淋在蛋上即可。

INGREDIENTS:

5		eggs
120g (¼ lb.)		shelled shrimp
3 T.		minced green onion
①	1 T.	cooking oil
	¼ t.	salt
②	½ c.	soup stock
	½ t.	cornstarch
	¼ t.	soy sauce
	pinch each of salt, MSG	

❶ Devein the shrimp, wash, drain, and set aside. Beat the eggs and set aside.

❷ Mix ① into the beaten egg (illus. 1). Heat in the microwave 2 minutes at 70% power. Remove (illus. 2) and set aside.

❸ Mix the shrimp with the minced green Onion and the egg mixture (illus. 3). Heat in the microwave 5 minutes at 70% power.

❹ Mix ② and heat 2 minutes in the microwave. Drizzle over the egg and serve.

蠔油扒雙菇

Mushrooms with Oyster Sauce

材料：

草菇	150公克	水	2大匙
洋菇罐頭		② 油	1大匙
	1罐（約580公克）	塩	¼小匙
青江菜	6棵	高湯	1杯
葱段	6段	③ 醬油、蠔油	
油	2大匙		各1大匙
① 水	¾杯	糖	2小匙
酒	1大匙	④ 水	2大匙
		太白粉	2小匙

❶草菇洗淨對切（圖1），入①料後加蓋入微波爐加熱
3分鐘，取出洗淨瀝乾備用。

❷洋菇罐頭去水（淨重400公克），洋菇漂水瀝乾備用。

❸青江菜洗淨對切（圖2），加②料入微波爐加熱4分
鐘，取出排盤。

❹油2大匙入微波爐預熱2分鐘，再爆香葱段1分30
秒，續入洋菇、草菇及③料（圖3），加蓋後加熱3
分鐘，入④料拌勻勾芡續熱1分鐘，即可取出排盤。

INGREDIENTS:

150g (⅓ lb.)	straw mushrooms
1 can	mushrooms (580g or 1⅓ lb.)
6 small bunches	ching kang tsai (or bok choy, or other similar leafy vegetable)
6 sections (1½'')	green onion
2 T.	cooking oil
① ¾ c.	water
1 T.	cooking wine
② 2 T.	water
1 T.	cooking oil
¼ t.	salt
③ 1 c.	soup stock
1 T. each:	soy sauce, oyster sauce
2 t.	sugar
④ 2 T.	water
2 t.	cornstarch

❶ Wash the straw mushrooms and cut in half
(illus. 1). Add ①, cover with plastic wrap,
and heat in the microwave 3 minutes.
Remove, wash, and drain. Set aside.

❷ Drain the canned mushrooms (net weight
400g or 14 oz.), soak briefly in water, and
drain again. Set aside.

❸ Wash the vegetable and cut each bunch
in half lengthwise (illus. 2). Add ② and
heat in the microwave 4 minutes. Remove
and arrange on a serving platter.

❹ Preheat 2 tablespoons oil in the microwave for 2 minutes, then fry the green
onion in the oil for 1 minute and 30
seconds. Add the canned mushrooms,
the straw mushrooms, and ③ (illus. 3).
Cover and heat 3 minutes in the microwave Mix in ④ and heat another minute
to thicken. Pour this mixture onto the
platter with the vegetable and serve.

香菇菜心

材料：

青江菜⋯⋯⋯⋯ 300公克	高湯⋯⋯⋯⋯⋯½杯
香菇⋯⋯⋯⋯⋯⋯⋯⋯	酒⋯⋯⋯⋯⋯½大匙
⋯⋯⋯⋯20公克(小8朵)	① 塩⋯⋯⋯⋯⋯¼小匙
油⋯⋯⋯⋯⋯⋯ 2大匙	胡椒粉、麻油⋯⋯⋯
葱段⋯⋯⋯⋯⋯ 6段	⋯⋯⋯⋯⋯各少許
	②太白粉、水⋯ 各1小匙

❶青江菜洗淨，大顆的對切成４份，小顆的對切成半
，香菇泡軟去蒂備用。

❷油２大匙預熱２分鐘，入香菇、葱段(圖１)加熱２
分鐘後，再入青江菜及①料，蓋上保鮮膜續熱４分
鐘後，取出排盤(圖２)，餘汁入②料勾芡加熱30秒
即可。

Chinese Mushrooms and Greens

INGREDIENTS:

300g (⅔ lb.)	ching kang tsai (or bok choy or other similar leafy **stalk vegetable**)
20g (⅔ oz.)	dried Chinese black mushrooms (about 8 small)
2 T.	cooking oil
6 sections (1½'')	**green onion**
① ½ c.	soup stock
½ T.	cooking wine
¼ t.	salt
pinch of pepper	
dash of sesame oil	
② 1 t. each:	cornstarch, water

❶ Wash the greens. Quarter lengthwise if using large
bunches; halve lengthwise if using small bunches.
Soak the mushrooms until soft and remove the stems.
Set aside.

❷ Preheat 2 tablespoons oil in the microwave for 2
minutes. Add the mushrooms and green onion (illus.
1). Heat in the microwave for 2 minutes. Add the
greens and ①. Cover with plastic wrap and heat for
4 minutes. Remove and arrange on a serving platter
(illus. 2). Add ② to the remaining liquid and heat 30
seconds to thicken. Serve.

6 人份
SERVES 6

芝麻金茸

Golden Mushrooms with Sesame Seeds

材料：

金菇	600公克		
黑芝麻	1½小匙	②	水 1大匙 太白粉 ½大匙

① 麻油 2大匙
薑汁 1大匙
塩 1小匙
味精 ¼小匙

❶ 黑芝麻置小碗中（圖1），蓋上保鮮膜入微波爐加熱1分鐘，取出備用。

❷ 金菇去老根（圖2），洗淨置盤中，入①料拌勻，蓋上保鮮膜，入微波爐加熱5分鐘，再入②料拌勻加熱30秒，取出灑上黑芝麻即可。

INGREDIENTS:

600g (1⅓ lb.)		golden mushrooms
1½ t.		black sesame seeds
①	2 T.	sesame oil
	1 T.	ginger root juice (use a lemon press)
	1 t.	salt
	¼ t.	MSG
②	1 T.	water
	½ T.	cornstarch

❶ Place the black sesame seeds in a small bowl (illus. 1) and cover with plastic wrap. Heat 1 minute in the microwave. Remove and set aside.

❷ Cut off the tough root portions from the golden mushrooms (illus. 2). Wash and place in a shallow bowl. Mix in ① and cover with plastic wrap. Heat 5 minutes in the microwave. Mix in ② and heat another 30 seconds. Remove, sprinkle the black sesame seeds over the top, and serve.

6人份
SERVES 6

 6人份
SERVES 6

82

干貝黃瓜

Cucumber with Dried Scallops

材料：

大黃瓜‥‥‥‥‥ 350公克	①	高湯‥‥‥‥‥‥½杯
干貝‥‥‥‥‥‥‥ 6個		塩‥‥‥‥‥‥¼小匙
	②太白粉、水‥ 各1小匙

❶干貝洗淨置小碗中加水１杯（圖１），蓋上保鮮膜後入微波爐加熱10分鐘，取出留汁½杯備用。

❷大黃瓜去皮切成2.5公分長段（共六段），用小湯匙挖出中央的籽（圖２），每個黃瓜中間鑲入一個蒸好的干貝（圖３），排在深盤中，淋上①料及干貝餘汁，加蓋加熱15分鐘後取出，將汁液倒在小碗內，拌入②料勾芡續熱30秒，淋在干貝黃瓜上即可。

■此道菜必須使用乾干貝。

INGREDIENTS:

350g (¾ lb.)	cucumber
6	dried scallops
① { ½ c.	soup stock
{ ¼ t.	salt
② 1 t. each:	cornstarch, water

❶ Wash the scallops and place in a small bowl. Add one cup of water (illus. 1). Cover with plastic wrap and heat in the microwave for 10 minutes. Remove from oven. Reserve ½ cup of the liquid.

❷ Peel the cucumber and cut into six 2.5 cm (1'') pieces. Scoop out the seeds in each piece with a small spoon (illus. 2). Insert a scallop inside each of the pieces (illus. 3). Arrange on a serving platter. Drizzle ① and the ½ cup of liquid from heating the scallops over the stuffed cucumbers. Cover and heat 15 minutes. Remove from the oven and pour off the liquid into a small bowl. Stir in ② and heat for 30 seconds to thicken. Pour over the stuffed cucumbers and serve.

■ Dried scallops rather than fresh are required for this recipe.

奶油菜膽

Scalloped Chinese Cabbage

材料：

大白菜	900公克
洋葱末	½杯
里肌肉	60公克
低筋麵粉	5大匙
奶水	½杯

①
薑	4片
水	½杯
塩	1½小匙
糖	¾小匙
味精	¼小匙

②
沙拉油	2大匙
奶油	1大匙

❶大白菜洗淨切粗塊，與①料拌勻後加蓋入微波爐加熱20分鐘取出，留汁½杯（圖1）備用，再瀝乾白菜（圖2）。

❷里肌肉切片備用。

❸②料入微波爐加熱2分鐘，入洋葱爆香1分30秒後，依序加入低筋麵粉、½杯白菜汁及奶水一起拌勻（圖3），再加入瀝乾的白菜及肉片入微波爐續熱20分鐘即可取出食用。

INGREDIENTS:

900g (2 lb.)	Chinese cabbage
½ c.	minced onion (about 70g or 2½ oz.)
60g (2 oz.)	lean pork
5 T.	low-gluten flour or cake flour
½ c.	milk

①
4 slices	ginger root
½ c.	water
1½ t.	salt
¾ t.	sugar
¼ t.	MSG

②
2 T.	cooking oil
1 T.	butter

❶ Wash the Chinese cabbage and cut into chunks. Mix together with ①, cover, and heat in the microwave for 20 minutes. Remove from oven and reserve ½ cup of the liquid (illus. 1), then drain the cabbage (illus. 2).

❷ Cut the pork into thin slices and set aside.

❸ Heat ② in the microwave for 2 minutes. Add the minced onion and heat for 1 minute and 30 seconds. Next add the flour, ½ cup reserved liquid from cooking the cabbage, and the milk until thoroughly blended (illus. 3). Finally, add the drained cabbage and the pork slices and heat in the microwave for 20 minutes. Serve.

清炒雙絲

Pork with String Beans

材料：

四季豆	200公克		油	1大匙
肉絲	70公克	②	塩	½小匙
			味精	⅛小匙

① 酒、油、水 各1大匙
醬油 2小匙
胡椒粉 少許

❶四季豆去頭尾，洗淨，斜切薄片（圖1）備用。
❷肉絲加①料拌醃10分鐘備用。
❸先將醃過的肉絲平鋪盤上（圖2），加熱1分鐘後，隨入四季豆及②料拌勻，蓋上保鮮膜續熱5分鐘即可。

INGREDIENTS:

200g (7 oz.)		green string beans
70g (2½ oz.)		pork, shredded
①	1 T. each:	cooking wine, cooking oil, water
	2 t.	soy sauce
	pinch of pepper	
②	1 T.	cooking oil
	½ t.	salt
	⅛ t.	MSG

❶ Snap the string beans, wash, and cut into thin slices at an angle, French-style (illus. 1). Set aside.
❷ Mix ① into the pork shreds and marinate for 10 minutes. Set aside.
❸ Spread the marinated pork shreds evenly over the bottom of a shallow bowl (illus. 2) and heat 1 minute. Then stir in the string beans and ②. Cover with plastic wrap and heat 5 minutes in the microwave. Serve.

6人份
SERVES 6

薑汁茄子

Gingered Eggplant

材料：

茄子·············· 370公克		醬油、薑末·············
葱末·············· 2大匙	①	············· 各1½大匙
水·············· 2杯		麻油·········· 1小匙
		味精·········· ¼小匙

❶茄子去皮切4公分長段（圖1），加水2杯，加蓋後加熱12分鐘，取出瀝乾水份，放入盤中蓋上保鮮膜（圖2），再放在冰箱內冰涼，食用前淋上①料，並灑上葱末即可。

■此道菜很合適在炎熱的夏天食用。

INGREDIENTS:

370g (13 oz.)	eggplant
2 T.	minced green onion
2 c.	water
① ⎰ 1½ T. each:	soy sauce, minced ginger root
⎱ 1 t.	sesame oil
¼ t.	MSG

❶ Peel the eggplant and cut into 4 cm (1⅔'') pieces (illus. 1). Place the eggplant in 2 cups of water, cover, and heat 12 minutes in the microwave. Remove and drain. Place in a shallow bowl, cover with plastic wrap (illus. 2), and allow to cool in the refrigerator. Sprinkle ① and some minced green onion over the top before serving.

■ This dish is particularly good in hot summer weather.

6人份
SERVES 6

清炒三絲

Vegetable Stir-Fry

材料：

綠豆芽	280公克		油	1½大匙
青椒	100公克	①	塩	½小匙
紅辣椒	1條		味精	⅛小匙

❶ 綠豆芽去頭尾（圖1），洗淨備用。
❷ 青椒及紅辣椒均去籽切絲備用。
❸ 將銀芽、青椒絲、紅辣椒絲及①料拌勻（圖2），蓋上保鮮膜後加熱2分30秒即可。

INGREDIENTS:

280g (10 oz.)		mung bean sprouts
100g (3½ oz.)		green pepper
1		small red chili pepper
①	1½ T.	cooking oil
	½ t.	salt
	⅛ t.	MSG

❶ Remove the ends from the bean sprouts (illus. 1; net weight will be about 9 oz. or 250g). Wash and set aside.
❷ Remove the seeds from the green pepper and red chili pepper and shred both. Set aside.
❸ Toss the bean sprouts, shredded green pepper, and shredded red chili pepper with ① until mixed (illus. 2). Cover with plastic wrap and heat in the microwave for 2 minutes and 30 seconds. Serve.

6人份
SERVES 6

干貝冬瓜

Wintermelon with Dried Scallops

材料：

冬瓜············· 750公克		水················ 5杯
干貝····· 30公克（約3粒）	①	塩··············· 1小匙
薑···················· 6片		味精··········· ¼小匙
油·················· 1大匙
水·················· 1杯
香菜·················少許

❶冬瓜去皮去籽，洗淨切1公分正方塊(圖1)備用。
❷干貝洗淨用水1杯泡30分鐘，使之泡軟(圖2)備用。
❸油1大匙入老薑加熱2分鐘，隨入冬瓜、干貝、干貝汁及①料，加蓋後加熱35分鐘，取出食前灑上少許香菜即可。

INGREDIENTS:

750g (1⅔ lb.)	wintermelon
30g (1 oz.)	dried scallops (about 3)
6 slices	ginger root
1 T.	cooking oil
1 c.	water
fresh coriander, as desired
① { 5 c.	water
1 t.	salt
¼ t.	MSG

❶ Peel the wintermelon, remove the seeds, and wash. Cut into 1 cm (½'') cubes (illus. 1). Set aside.
❷ Wash the dried scallops and soak in 1 cup of water for 30 minutes, until soft (illus. 2). Set aside.
❸ Add the ginger root to 1 tablespoon oil and heat 2 minutes in the microwave. Add the wintermelon, scallops, water from soaking the scallops, and ①. Cover and heat 35 minutes. Sprinkle a little fresh coriander over the top before serving.

6人份
SERVES 6

6 人份
SERVES 6

餛 飩 湯 / Wonton Soup

材料：

絞肉··············	110公克
芹菜··············	75公克
餛飩皮··············	24張
油··············	2大匙
紅葱頭（切末）······	1大匙
熱開水··············	6杯

①
蛋白··············	¼個
葱末·······	1½小匙
薑末··········	1小匙
塩··············	⅜小匙
味精、酒、麻油······ 各¼小匙	
胡椒粉········	⅛小匙

②
塩··········	1½小匙
味精、麻油·········· 各¼小匙	
胡椒粉········	⅛小匙

❶芹菜洗淨切末備用。
❷絞肉調入①料拌勻成餡，分成24等份（圖1）備用。
❸每張餛飩皮包入1份餡（圖2）即成餛飩（圖3）。
❹大湯碗內入油2大匙，預熱3分鐘後，入紅葱頭爆香1分30秒，隨入6杯熱開水、②料及餛飩，續熱2分30秒，取出灑上芹菜末即成餛飩湯。
■這道菜若當點心食用，可以小白菜150公克代替芹菜末，但最後必須再加熱30秒，將小白菜煮熟。

INGREDIENTS:

110g (¼ lb.)	ground pork
75g (2½ oz.)	celery, preferably Chinese
24	wonton wrappers
2 T.	cooking oil
1 T.	minced shallot
6 c.	hot water

①
¼	egg white
1½ t.	minced green onion
1 t.	minced ginger
⅜ t.	salt
¼ t. each:	MSG, cooking wine, sesame oil
⅛ t.	pepper

②
1½ t.	salt
¼ t. each:	MSG, sesame oil
⅛ t.	pepper

❶ Wash the celery, mince, and set aside.
❷ Mix ① into the ground pork to make the filling. Divide into 24 equal portions (illus. 1) and set aside.
❸ Wrap one portion of filling inside each of the 24 wonton wrappers (illus. 2) to make the wontons (illus. 3).
❹ Add 2 tablespoons oil to a large soup bowl and preheat 3 minutes in the microwave. Fry the minced shallot in the oil 1 minute and 30 seconds. Add the 6 cups of water, ②, and the wontons. Heat 2 minutes and 30 seconds. Sprinkle the minced celery over the top of the soup. Serve.

■ If served as a snack, wash and chop 150g (⅓ lb.) Chinese cabbage to replace the minced celery. Heat the soup with the chopped cabbage an extra 30 seconds or so to cook the cabbage.

哈蜜瓜盅

Chicken Soup in Whole Cantaloupe

材料：

哈蜜瓜‥‥‥‥‥‥‥‥‥‥
‥‥‥‥ 1個（約1500公克）
雞胸肉‥‥‥‥‥ 120公克
香菇‥‥‥‥‥‥ 1朵（大）
干貝‥‥‥‥‥‥‥‥‥ ½個
薑‥‥‥‥‥‥‥‥‥‥ 2片
水‥‥‥‥‥‥‥‥‥‥ 1杯

① { 高湯‥‥‥‥ 1¼杯
     酒‥‥‥‥‥ 1小匙
     塩‥‥‥‥‥ ¼小匙 }

❶雞胸肉切0.5公分正方塊，香菇泡軟去蒂切0.5公分
  見方，薑片切絲備用。
❷干貝洗淨放小碗內，入1杯水加熱5分鐘，取出用
  手撕成絲（圖1），餘¾杯干貝蒸汁留用。
❸哈蜜瓜洗淨，於蒂頭處切一個蓋子（圖2），用湯匙
  挖出部份果肉（圖3），成爲盅狀，加入雞肉、香菇
  、薑絲、干貝、干貝汁及①料，將蒂頭蓋子蓋回，
  加熱12分鐘即可。

INGREDIENTS:

1	cantaloupe (about 1500g or 3⅓ lb.)
120g (⅓ lb.)	chicken breast meat
1	large dried Chinese black mushroom
½	dried scallop
2 slices	ginger root
1 c.	water

① { 1¼ c.   soup stock
     1 t.   cooking wine
     ¼ t.   salt }

❶ Cut the chicken into 0.5 cm (¼'') cubes. Soak the dried Chinese black mushroom until soft, remove the stem, and cut into 0.5 cm (¼'') cubes. Shred the ginger root slices. Set aside.

❷ Wash the ½ dried scallop and place in a small bowl. Add 1 cup water and heat 5 minutes in the microwave. Remove the scallop from the bowl and tear into shreds (illus. 1). Save ¾ cup of the liquid left from cooking the scallop.

❸ Wash the cantaloupe and cut out a cover on the top (stem) end (illus. 2). Scoop out the seeds and discard, then scoop out some of the fruit (illus. 3) to form a bowl. Add the chicken, mushroom, shredded ginger root, scallop, the liquid from cooking the scallop, and ①. Replace the cover cut from the cantaloupe and heat 12 minutes in the microwave. Serve.

榨菜肉絲細粉湯

Pork Shred and Pickled Mustard Soup

材料：

榨菜	60公克		開水	5杯
肉絲	50公克		塩	1小匙
粉絲	1把	②	麻油	½小匙
葱末	2大匙		味精	⅛小匙
水	1杯		胡椒粉	少許

① ┌ 水 ⋯⋯⋯ 1大匙
　 │ 醬油 ⋯⋯⋯ 1小匙
　 └ 塩 ⋯⋯⋯ ⅛小匙

❶ 榨菜略洗切絲（圖1），加水1杯浸泡5分鐘後瀝乾備用。

❷ 肉絲入①料拌醃備用。

❸ 粉絲用開水浸泡20分鐘，再瀝乾切段（圖2）備用。

❹ 粉絲入②料加熱2分鐘後隨入肉絲、榨菜絲（圖3），續熱1分鐘，取出灑上葱末即可。

■ ②料中的開水若換成冷水，其加熱時間必須加長15分鐘。

INGREDIENTS:

60g (2 oz.)		Szechuan pickled mustard greens (cha tsai)
50g (1⅔ oz.)		shredded pork
1 bunch		dry bean thread
2 T.		minced green onion
1 c.		water
①	1 T.	water
	1 t.	soy sauce
	⅛ t.	salt
②	5 c.	water
	1 t.	salt
	½ t.	sesame oil
	⅛ t.	MSG
	pinch of pepper	

❶ Rinse the Szechuan pickled mustard greens and shred (illus. 1). Soak 5 minutes in 1 cup of water. Drain and set aside.

❷ Mix ① into the shredded pork and set aside.

❸ Soak the bean thread in water for 20 minutes. Drain, cut into short lengths (illus. 2), and set aside.

❹ Add ② to the bean thread and heat 2 minutes in the microwave. Add the shredded pork and shredded pickled mustard greens (illus. 3) and heat 1 minute in the microwave. Sprinkle the minced green onion over the top and serve.

■ If cold water is used in ②, add 15 minutes to the cooking time.

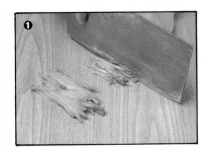

芥菜燉雞

Stewed Chicken with Mustard Green

材料：

雞…… 半隻（約600公克）		
芥菜…………… 300公克	①	水………………… 6杯
薑………………12片		塩………… 1¼小匙

❶ 芥菜洗淨切粗塊（圖1）備用。

❷ 雞洗淨剁與芥菜同等大小之塊狀，入微波爐加熱３
分鐘，取出再次洗淨去血水，放入大碗內加芥菜、
薑片（圖2）及①料，加蓋並加熱50分鐘即可。

Stewed Chicken with Mustard Green

INGREDIENTS:

½	chicken (about 600g or 1⅓ lb.)
300g (⅔ lb.)	mustard greens
12 slices	ginger root
① ⎰ 6 c.	water
⎱ 1¼ t.	salt

❶ Wash the mustard greens and cut into medium pieces (illus. 1). Set aside.

❷ Wash the chicken and cut into chunks about the same size as the mustard greens. Heat the chicken 3 minutes in the microwave. Wash and drain the bloody liquid. Place in a large bowl together with the mustard greens, ginger root (illus. 2), and ①. Cover, heat 50 minutes, and serve.

6人份
SERVES 6

冬瓜肉丸湯

Wintermelon and Meatball Soup

材料：

冬瓜……………450公克
絞肉……………150公克
韮黃末……………2大匙

① 葱末…………1大匙
醬油、酒…各1小匙
麻油、太白粉………
……………各½小匙
塩、胡椒粉…………
……………各¼小匙
味精…………⅛小匙

② 塩……………¾小匙
味精…………⅛小匙
水………………6杯

❶絞肉加①料拌勻後甩打數次(圖1)，做成12個肉丸備用。

❷冬瓜去皮去籽(淨重約300公克)，切約1公分正方塊，洗淨放入大碗內(圖2)，加②料加蓋後加熱10分鐘，入肉丸續熱10分鐘，取出灑上韮黃末即可。

6人份
SERVES 6

INGREDIENTS:

450g (1 lb.)	wintermelon
150g (⅓ lb.)	ground pork
2 T.	minced yellow Chinese chives
① 1 T.	minced green onion
① 1 t. each:	soy sauce, cooking wine
① ½ t. each:	sesame oil, cornstarch
① ¼ t. each:	salt, pepper
① ⅛ t.	MSG
② ¾ t.	salt
② ⅛ t.	MSG
② 6 c.	water

❶ Mix ① into the ground pork, form into a ball, and throw against a counter or cutting board several times (to improve the texture; illus. 1). Make into 12 meatballs and set aside.

❷ Peel the wintermelon and remove the seeds (net weight will be about 300g or ⅔ lb.) Cut into about 1 cm (½") cubes, wash, and place in a large bowl (illus. 2). Add ②, cover, and heat 10 minutes in the microwave. Add the meatballs and heat another 10 minutes. Sprinkle the minced yellow Chinese chives (or substitute minced green onion) over the top and serve.

椰茸糯米球 / Coconut Rice Balls

材料：

元宵粉	1½杯	①	細糖	2½大匙
椰子粉、沸水	各¾杯		豬油、水	各2大匙
澄粉	¼杯			
紅豆沙	240公克			
櫻桃	1個			
冷水	5杯			

❶ 紅豆沙分成24份並搓成圓球狀備用。

❷ 澄粉用¾杯的沸水燙熟（圖1），再與元宵粉及①料拌勻，取其中40公克壓成麵餅狀（圖2）備用。

❸ 水1杯入微波爐預熱2分鐘，入麵餅（圖3）續熱1分鐘，取出再與剩餘的❷料揉勻，分成24份（每份約18〜20公克）外皮。

❹ 每份外皮包入1份豆沙餡成糯米球。

❺ 水4杯入微波爐加熱5分鐘，再入12個做好的糯米球，加熱4分鐘，即可取出沾上椰子粉。

❻ 剩餘的12個糯米球入原有熱水中續熱4分鐘，取出沾上椰子粉，每個糯米球以櫻桃裝飾排盤。

Coconut Rice Balls

INGREDIENTS:

1½ c.	glutinous rice flour (mochi flour; sweet rice flour)
¾ c. each:	desiccated (or flaked) coconut, boiling water
¼ c.	wheat starch
240g (8½ oz.)	sweet red (adzuki) bean paste
1	maraschino cherry
5 c.	cold water
① 2½ T.	white sugar
2 T. each:	lard, water

❶ Divide the red bean paste into 24 equal portions and roll each into a ball. Set aside.

❷ Add ¾ cup boiling water to the wheat starch (illus. 1). Mix in the glutinous rice flour and ① until well blended. Make about 40g (1⅓ oz.) of the dough into a pancake shape (illus. 2) and set aside.

❸ Preheat 1 cup of the water in the microwave for 2 minutes. Add the dough "pancake" (illus. 3) and heat for another minute in the microwave. Remove the "pancake" and knead it together with the remaining dough. Divide into 24 equal portions (about 20g or ⅔ oz. each). These are for the outer layer of the coconut rice balls.

❹ Wrap each of the portions of dough around a red bean paste ball, smoothing it into a ball.

❺ Heat 4 cups of water in the microwave for 5 minutes. Add 12 of the filled rice balls and heat 4 minutes. Remove and roll in the coconut.

❻ Place the remaining 12 rice balls in the same bowl of water and heat for 4 minutes in the microwave. Remove and roll in coconut. Garnish each of the coconut rice balls with a bit of maraschino cherry and arrange on a serving plate.

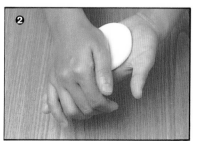

馬 拉 糕 / Chinese Sponge Cake

材料：

雞蛋	3個	奶水	½杯
白砂糖	½杯	② 油	¼杯
玻璃紙	1張	水	2大匙

① { 低筋麵粉 …… 1½杯
    泡打粉 ……… 1大匙
    香草片(壓碎) … 2片

❶ 將①料過篩(圖1)，模型內加玻璃紙(圖2)備用。

❷ 將雞蛋的蛋黃與蛋白分開，蛋白加砂糖，用直型打蛋器打至硬性發泡，再依序加入蛋黃、過篩後之①料及②料，並用橡皮刮刀攪拌均勻後，倒入已鋪好玻璃紙之模型內(圖3)，入微波爐加熱6分鐘即可。

INGREDIENTS:

	3	eggs
	½ c.	sugar
	1 sheet	cellophane
①	{ 1½ c.	low-gluten flour or cake flour
	1 T.	baking powder
②	{ ¼ t.	vanilla extract
	½ c.	milk
	¼ c.	cooking oil
	2 T.	water

❶ Sift ① together (illus. 1). Line a baking pan with cellophane (illus. 2) and set aside.

❷ Separate the egg. Add the sugar to the egg white and beat with an egg beater until stiff peaks form. To this mixture add, in the following order, the egg yolk, ①, and ②, then fold together with a spatula until blended. Pour the batter into the cellophane-lined baking pan (illus. 3) and heat in the microwave for 6 minutes. Serve.

什錦炒飯

材料：

蓬萊米⋯⋯⋯⋯⋯⋯ 3杯	豬肉丁⋯⋯ 100公克
乾蝦米⋯⋯⋯⋯⋯30公克	毛豆⋯⋯⋯⋯80公克 ①
香菇⋯⋯⋯⋯⋯ 1朵(大)	紅蘿蔔丁⋯⋯30公克
油⋯⋯⋯⋯⋯⋯ 4大匙	酒⋯⋯⋯⋯ 2小匙
	塩、醬油⋯⋯⋯⋯⋯ ②
	⋯⋯⋯⋯各1½小匙
	味精⋯⋯⋯⋯½小匙

❶米洗淨後加水2½杯，泡約30分鐘(圖1)備用。
❷香菇用熱水泡軟去蒂切丁，乾蝦米洗淨備用。
❸油4大匙預熱2分鐘後，爆香香菇丁及乾蝦米3分鐘(圖2)取出與①、②料及泡過水的米一起拌勻(圖3)，加蓋加熱25分鐘後，靜置爐內以餘熱燜5分鐘再取出即可。

Little-of-Everything Fried Rice

INGREDIENTS:

3 c.		short grain rice
30g (1 oz.)		small dried shrimp
1		large dried Chinese black mushroom
4 T.		cooking oil
①	100g (3½ oz.)	diced pork
	80g (2¾ oz.)	fresh soybeans or peas
	30g (1 oz.)	diced carrot
②	2 t.	cooking wine
	1½ t. each:	salt, soy sauce
	½ t.	MSG

❶ Wash the rice, drain, then add 2½ cups water to it. Soak for about 30 minutes (illus. 1). Set aside.

❷ Soak the mushroom in water until soft. Remove the stem and discard. Dice the mushroom. Wash the dried shrimp. Set aside.

❸ Preheat 4 tablespoons oil in the microwave for 2 minutes. Fry the diced mushrooms and the small dried shrimp in the oil for 3 minutes (illus. 2). Remove and mix in ①, ②, and the soaked rice until well combined (illus. 3). Cover and heat 25 minutes in the microwave. Leave in the microwave undisturbed for 5 minutes after the power shuts off. Serve.

蜜餞薯條

Candy-Coated Yams

材料：
紅心蕃薯…1斤（600公克）
白芝麻（炒過）…… 1大匙

① ⎧ 水………… 1½杯
⎪ 麥芽糖…… 5大匙
⎨ 糖………… 2大匙
⎪ 白醋……… ½小匙
⎩ 塩……… 少許

❶蕃薯洗淨去皮切長條狀（圖1）備用。
❷將蕃薯塊及①料拌勻（圖2），入微波爐加熱30分，
　至汁成黏稠狀即可取出灑上白芝麻。

INGREDIENTS:
600g (1⅓ lb.)   yams
1 T.   white sesame seeds,
         toasted

① ⎧ 1½ c.   water
⎪ 5 T.   malt syrup
⎨ 2 T.   white sugar
⎪ ½ t.   white rice vinegar
⎩ dash of salt

❶ Wash the yams, peel, and cut into lang stnips (illus. 1). Set aside.
❷ Mix ① into the yams (illus. 2). Heat for 30 minutes in the microwave, until the liquid becomes thick and sticky. Sprinkle on the toasted white sesame seeds and serve.

芋 泥

Sweet Taro Paste

材料：
芋頭……………… 800公克
①
豬油……………½杯
水………………½杯
糖……………… 6大匙
柳丁皮末…… 1大匙

❶芋頭去皮洗淨切粗片（圖1）（淨重約600公克），置碗
內加蓋入微波爐加熱10分鐘，取出壓成泥（圖2）備
用。

❷將①料與芋泥拌勻，加蓋後加熱6分鐘即可趁熱供
食。

INGREDIENTS:
800g (1¾ lb.)   taro (dasheen)
①
½ c.   lard
½ c.   water
6 T.   sugar
1 T.   grated orange peel

❶ Peel the taros, wash, and cut into thick slices
(illus. 1; net weight will be about 1⅓ lb. or 600
g). Place in a bowl, cover, and heat in the
microwave for 10 minutes. Remove and mash
into a smooth paste (illus. 2). Set aside.

❷ Mix ① into the taro paste until well blended.
Cover and heat 6 minutes in the microwave.
Serve hot.

6人份
SERVES 6

胡蘿蔔蛋糕

Carrot Cake

材料：

油‧‧‧‧‧‧‧‧‧‧‧‧‧‧‧‧‧‧‧‧少許

① 高筋麵粉‧‧‧‧‧ 2½杯
泡打粉‧‧‧‧‧‧‧ 1大匙
肉桂粉‧‧‧‧‧‧‧‧ 2小匙
小蘇打、豆蔻粉、塩
‧‧‧‧‧‧‧‧‧‧‧‧ 各1小匙

② 黑糖‧‧‧‧‧‧‧‧‧‧‧ 1杯
細砂糖、油‧‧‧各¾杯
蛋‧‧‧‧‧‧‧‧‧‧‧‧‧ 4個

③ 胡蘿蔔末‧‧‧ 450公克
罐頭鳳梨丁‧‧‧‧‧‧‧‧‧
‧‧‧‧‧‧‧‧‧‧‧ 200公克
核桃末‧‧‧‧‧‧‧‧‧‧½杯

❶將①料全部過篩備用。模型內先抹少許油（圖１）備用。

❷②料用直型打蛋器打５分鐘，分次加入過篩後的①料（圖２）拌勻，再入③料也攪拌均勻，最後倒入已抹油的模型內以80％電力加熱22分鐘即可。

INGREDIENTS:

cooking oil, as needed

① 2½ c.   high-gluten or all-purpose flour
1 T.   baking powder
2 t.   ground cinnamon
1 t. each: baking soda, nutmeg, salt

② 1 c.   brown sugar
¾ c. each: white sugar, cooking oil
4   eggs

③ 450g (1 lb.)   carrots
200g (7 oz.)   canned crushed pineapple
½ c.   chopped walnuts

❶ Sift ① together and set aside. Oil a cake pan (illus. 1) and set aside.

❷ Beat ② for 5 minutes. Pour a small amount at a time into ① (illus. 2), mixing thoroughly each time, until it is all combined. Stir in ③ until blended. Pour the batter into the oiled cake pan. Bake in the microwave for 22 minutes at 80% power. Serve.

12人份
SERVES 12

味全家政班

Wei-Chuan Cooking School

味全家政班創立於民國五十年，經過三十餘年的努力，它不只是國內歷史最悠久的家政研習班，更成爲一所正式學制之外的專門學校。

創立之初，味全家政班以教授中國菜及研習烹飪技術爲主，因教學成果良好，備受各界讚譽，乃於民國五十二年，增闢插花、工藝、美容等各門專科，精湛的師資，教學內容的充實，深獲海內外的肯定與好評。

三十餘年來，先後來班參與研習的學員已近二十萬人次，學員的足跡遍及台灣以外，更有許多國外的團體或個人專程抵台，到味全家政班求教，在習得中國菜烹調的精髓後，或返回居住地經營餐飲業，或擔任家政教師，或獲聘爲中國餐廳主廚者大有人在，成就倍受激賞。

近年來，味全家政班亟力研究開發改良中國菜餚，並深入國際間，採集各種精緻、道地美食，除了樹立中華文化「食的精神」外，並將各國烹飪口味去蕪存菁，擷取地方特色。爲了確保這些研究工作更加落實，我們特將這些集合海內外餐飲界與研發單位的精典之作，以縝密的拍攝技巧與專業編輯，出版各式食譜，以做傳承。

薪傳與發揚中國烹飪的藝術，是味全家政班一貫的理念，日後，也將秉持宗旨，永續不輟。

Since its establishment in 1961, Wei-Chuan Cooking School has made a continuous commitment toward improving and modernizing the culinary art of cooking and special skills training. As a result, it is the oldest and most successful school of its kind in Taiwan.

In the beginning, Wei-Chuan Cooking School was primarily teaching and researching Chinese cooking techniques. However, due to popular demand, the curriculum was expanded to cover courses in flower arrangements, handcrafts, beauty care, dress making and many other specialized fields by 1963.

The fact that almost 200,000 students, from Taiwan and other countries all over the world, have matriculated in this school can be directly attributed to the high quality of the teaching staff and the excellent curriculum provided to the studen t's. Many of the graduates have become successful restaurant owners and chefs, and in numerous cases, respected teachers.

While Wei-Chuan Cooking School has always been committed to developing and improving Chinese cuisine, we have recently extended our efforts toward gathering information and researching recipes from d ifferent provinces of China. With the same dedication to accuracy and perfection as always, we have begun to publish these authentic regional gourmet recipes for our devoted readers. These new publications will continue to reflect the fine tradition of quality our public has grown to appreciate and expect.

純青出版社

劃撥帳號：12106299
電　　話：(○二)五○八四三三一
傳　　真：(○二)五○七四九○二
地　　址：台北市松江路125號５樓

健康食譜
- 100道菜
- 120頁
- 中英對照

Healthful Cooking
- 100 recipes
- 120 pages
- Chinese/English Bilingual

素食
- 84道菜
- 120頁
- 中英對照

Vegetarian Cooking
- 84 recipes
- 120 pages
- Chinese/English Bilingual

微波食譜第一冊
- 62道菜
- 112頁
- 中英對照

Microwave Cooking Chinese Style
- 62 recipes
- 112 pages
- Chinese/English Bilingual

微波食譜第二冊
- 76道菜
- 128頁
- 中英對照

Microwave Cooking Chinese Style 2
- 76 recipes
- 128 pages
- Chinese/English Bilingual

飲茶食譜
- 88道菜
- 128頁
- 中英對照

Chinese Dim Sum
- 88 recipes
- 128 pages
- Chinese/English Bilingual

美味小菜
- 92道菜
- 96頁
- 中英對照

Appetizers
- 92 recipes
- 96 pages
- Chinese/English Bilingual

實用烘焙
- 77道點心
- 96頁
- 中英對照

International Baking Delight
- 77 recipes
- 96 pages
- Chinese/English Bilingual

四川菜
- 115道菜
- 96頁
- 中英對照

Chinese Cuisine Szechwan Style
- 115 recipes
- 96 pages
- Chinese/English Bilingual

上海菜
- 91道菜
- 96頁
- 中英對照

Chinese Cuisine Shanghai Style
- 91 recipes
- 96 pages
- Chinese/English Bilingual

台灣菜
- 73道菜
- 120頁
- 中英對照

Chinese Cuisine Taiwanese Style
- 73 recipes
- 120 pages
- Chinese/English Bilingual

Chin-Chin Publishing

h fl., 125 Sung Chiang Rd.,Taipei 104, Taiwan, R.O.C

el : (02)5084331 Fax : (02)5074902

麵食-家常篇
- 91 道菜
- 96 頁
- 中英對照

Noodles Home Cooking
- 91 recipes
- 96 pages
- Chinese/English Bilingual

麵食-精華篇
- 87 道菜
- 96 頁
- 中英對照

Noodles Classical Cooking
- 87 recipes
- 96 pages
- Chinese/English Bilingual

米食-家常篇
- 84 道菜
- 96 頁
- 中英對照

Rice Home Cooking
- 84 recipes
- 96 pages
- Chinese/English Bilingual

米食-傳統篇
- 82 道菜
- 96 頁
- 中英對照

Rice Traditional Cooking
- 82 recipes
- 96 pages
- Chinese/English Bilingual

家常100
- 100 道菜
- 96 頁
- 中英對照

Favorite Chinese Dishes
- 100 recipes
- 96 pages
- Chinese/English Bilingual

養生藥膳
- 73 道菜
- 128 頁
- 中英對照

Chinese Herb Cooking for Health
- 73 recipes
- 128 pages
- Chinese/English Bilingual

健康素
- 76 道菜
- 96 頁
- 中英對照

Simply Vegetarian
- 76 recipes
- 96 pages
- Chinese/English Bilingual

營養便當
- 147 道菜
- 96 頁
- 中文版

嬰幼兒食譜
- 140 道菜
- 104 頁
- 中文版

家常菜
- 226 道菜
- 200 頁
- 中文版

庖廚偏方　庖廚錦囊　庖廚樂
- 中文版

想要追求精緻的口味感受？ **開**

就有

味全冷凍調理食品

您看到的這一桌豐富美味的大餐，全都是味全以冷凍調理食品為您料理的哦！味全冷調是由味全家政班以獨家研究的配方精心調製即使最挑剔的嘴，也會讚不絕口，再加上口味繁多，不論您想吃什麼，只有味全冷凍調理食品最能滿足您追求多樣美味的需求，選擇味全，相信您會滿意。

 味全冷凍調理食品均榮獲CAS優良冷凍食品双標誌。

味全消費者服務中心電話：080-221007

豬肉水餃　　菲菜水餃　　素食水餃　　斤裝貢丸　　鮮肉包　　　炸鷄塊　　　鮮肉雲吞　菜肉雲吞

醬油中的天之美"露"
——味全醬油露

以100％純黃豆釀造的味全醬
油露，甘、醇、香、濃，風
味自然。
醬油中的真正好醬油——味
全醬油露。
煎、煮、炒、炸、沾樣樣精
彩。

味全醬油露